Touching the Trees

By Jennifer McBride

Published in the United States by:
CCS Communications, LLC.
www.ccs-comm.com

Copyright © Jennifer McBride, 2011
All rights reserved

ISBN-13: 978-1456353575
ISBN-10: 1456353578

Printed in the United States of America
by CreateSpace

No part of this book may be reproduced or transmitted in any form or by any means, either electronic or mechanical, including but not limited to photocopying, recording, or up-loading, without permission in writing from the publisher. Please purchase only authorized electronic editions and do not participate or encourage electronic piracy of copyrighted materials. Your support of the author's rights is appreciated.

Author photograph © Flash Digital Portraits
Cover photograph © Jennifer McBride
Chapter heading photograph © John McNamara

For my saplings and sequoias,
You know who you are…

In memory of Barbara Bean

Smile when you want to.
Cry when you need to.
Laugh whenever possible.
- J McB

Touching the Trees

*For Geri —
Your daughter
is awesome!*

Jenn

Reader Reactions

There is so much for anyone to learn from in this book, as well as to examine in his or her own life. I can only imagine the brilliantly glowing smiles that are cast down on her from her guardian angel. [Jennifer McBride] is an absolute inspiration. Plain and simple.
 —Jennifer B., Michigan

This book is just a wonderful look into life during and after those dark days [of transition].
 —Greta K., Minneapolis

Jennifer McBride shared many things we all struggle with, and she did it bravely and openly.
 —Pastor Therese Helker, Grace Lutheran Church, Apple Valley, Minnesota

As women, our relationships have a tendency to define us for better or worse. Jennifer has artfully described this journey of becoming a mature, personally successful woman with humor, grace, and an honest interpretation of her experience.
 —Shannon H., Missouri

I really can relate to and appreciate the pure and raw emotion that she shares in her story. I walk to the beat of my own drum, so I value the importance of not being labeled.
 —Jill T., Indiana

Table of Contents

Part I. Waking Up

1. Bad Things and Braveheart..........................1
2. My Cousin Betsy................................13
3. Old Ladies....................................21
4. Labels and Boxes..............................29
5. Diamond Rings and Padded Bras.............37
6. Touching the Trees, Part 1....................49

Part II. Looking Up

7. Abortion and the Egg Farmer's Daughter 58
8. Arrows, Downward and Up 67
9. Battleship....................................77
10. Yeses and Nos................................83
11. Mine...91
12. Mirrors......................................97
13. Plastic Bags 107
14. The Doorway Out............................117
15. Traveling by Anger..........................123

16. Thunder and Silence 133

Part III. Showing Up

17. The Replacement 140

18. Worlds Colliding 149

19. The Tent Caterpillar 157

20. My Hero-Worshipping Moth 165

21. Hanging Light Fixtures 171

22. Base Frequency and the Emotional Doppler Effect 177

23. The Language of Us 187

24. Sorry is an Easy Word to Hate 195

25. The Ease of Ordinary Things 201

Part IV. Standing Up

26. Walls and Bridges 206

27. Superfamily 215

28. The Last Jalapeno 221

29. Hay Pillows and Splat Corners 229

30. Tubing the Wake 237

31. The Fly on the Airplane 243

32. The Carousel 253

33. Nine or None 261

34. Strings 269

35. Weed Killer 277

36. Water Weight 285

37. Touching the Trees, Part 2 293

Introduction

This book isn't actually a metaphor (since it's actually a book), but it's a collection of stories and metaphors that have guided me through a transition from there to *here*. This book also isn't a step-by-step manual for how to get from there to *there*—that other place we might want to be, that life we dream about in rare quiet moments. There aren't any checklists or prescriptions or guaranteed plans.

What this book is, though, is a gentle knock on your door when you've been longing for company. It's a pair of binoculars when the eagle is just out of view. It's a signpost, a beacon, or a warm blanket. It's a reminder that we aren't alone and *we have what it takes*.

I didn't have the time or good fortune to travel the world to find myself so I had to look much closer to home—at the lessons I could learn from my daily life and my ordinary travails. Epiphanies don't have to happen in a shrine or on a sabbatical. They can happen in a kitchen, car, or bedroom and at any time. They can happen to you whether you're on a journey or in quiet contemplation.

So I'd like to tell you a story. It's the story of a life that wasn't always what it could have or should have been. But it's also the story of a life that has become more than I ever thought would be possible just a few years ago.

We all have the power to fight fear and complacency. We gain that power by learning lessons from the stories that present themselves to us. Maybe this book will boost your strength to start or continue on your journey. Better yet, maybe it will inspire you to look and listen for lessons in your particular circumstances.

No matter what, though, know this. If I can do it, you can do it. I believe in you.

Part I.
Waking Up

Chapter One
Bad Things and Braveheart

I've spent some time wondering where this story starts. It would be easy to say that it starts with a divorce, but a divorce is always a product of circumstances and breakdowns that came before it.

So I thought maybe it started with a wedding, but the wedding was simply a product of expectations and hopes that came before *it*.

It didn't really start with a trauma in college or any of the normal drama in high school. It also didn't start in Mrs. Lark's third grade classroom, although my love of words certainly did.

Touching the Trees

So I went all the way back and realized that this story starts on the day my Great Aunt Cate's mother died.

Because it was also the day I was born.

For a long time, my Great Aunt Cate thought I was the reincarnation of her dead mother.

I didn't know Aunt Cate very well. She was my grandfather's brother's wife and her mother was no relation at all. But the coincidence of my birth and her death made enough sense to Aunt Cate that she never failed to mention it to me on those rare occasions that we saw each other at family reunions.

Back then I was too young to understand the meaning of "identity" or to know how important it would someday be to figure out my own. I had no way of comprehending how lucky I was that I'd never met Aunt Cate's mother—because even then I was someone who would have pulled that woman's persona on like a costume cape.

Growing up, I changed identities like a child-sized chameleon. For years I believed that I was part Blackfoot Indian and crept around the house, practicing silent heel-toe walking to better be able to sneak food during my parents' bridge parties. I stepped into my birth-order expectations (as expected, since I was the eldest) and honed my family talents (music from one side, athletics from the other). Each school year or summer break was a chance to re-make myself into someone that seemed more like who I should be.

The problem was, while I was usually pretty good at figuring out whom I *should* be, it never felt quite like it was who I *was*.

After all, a costume was just a costume.

I'm not ashamed to say that I didn't go down the path of finding my true self alone. As much as I wish I could have whipped off my mom jeans, appliqued sweatshirts, cocktail dresses, work suits, or any other accoutrement I wore during my life with my own super-woman strength, I just couldn't.

So I turned to a very few very close friends and some family, all who did a great job listening and empathizing in between their own crazy busy lives. But I knew I needed more help than I could reasonably ask any of them for.

Luckily I found someone who could bolster my quivering arms and calm my hyper-pounding heart, although sometimes that support took the form of firm, yet figurative, shoulder shakes.

His name is Zane. He's the greatest therapist in the world, although he didn't start out that way. But more on that later…

A couple of years ago, I left my Wednesday therapy session with Zane with two assignments. For those people not familiar with therapy, "assignments" are therapy-speak for "Quit your complaining and help yourself for once in your pathetic, co-dependent life." Okay, maybe it's not an exact representation, but that's what assignments feel like on a particularly low day. They are exercises that you should do (but don't have to, of course!) to solve whatever problem has brought you to therapy in the first place. They are important personal growth stepping stones to self-actualization. As much as I sometimes resisted them, I knew they were important for me to do if I was committed to seeking my true identity.

Early on in therapy, I needed assignments to keep me focused on finding myself—even if they were designed to make me try being someone different for a little bit.

Anyway, my assignments that day were 1) Watch the movie *Braveheart*, and 2) Do a Bad Thing.

Huh?

Here was the premise of Assignment #1, I think: Watch *Braveheart* to learn about freedom and to what extent someone will go to protect it. I had been whining for months about not having emotional freedom, so I suspect this assignment was Zane's knee-jerk reaction to, "If she complains about freedom ONE MORE TIME...."

Assignment #2 was: Do a bad thing to overcome an unrealistic fear of getting in trouble. As a side note, when he asked me to write down every bad thing I'd ever done...well, let's just say the list wasn't very long and he was yawning the entire time.

Before I left the couch, Zane tried to give me suggestions of bad things to do. "Cut in line," he said. "Don't use a turn signal." "Ignore someone." "Just don't rob --"

"Steal—" I said over him.

"A bank," he finished.

"A car," I added. So we were on the same wavelength. Do something bad, but not something so illegal that it would put his professional liability policy in jeopardy of being invoked. "Sorry, Officer, but my therapist TOLD me to." After I left, I wondered if Zane put his head in his hands and rolled it back and forth, mumbling, "That was dumb. Really, really dumb. My insurance premiums are going to go WAY up."

Because my previous list of bad things was so meager and malnourished, I decided to overcompensate and plan something bad for every day between then and my session the next week. I'd save *Braveheart* for the end so I would have a little time to borrow it, rent it, or just read the summary online.

So that Wednesday, after my session, I went to lunch, not using my turn signal almost the whole time, except for when I passed churches…and schools…and the police station. I contemplated not saying "Thank you" to the stocky guy serving me noodles and broccoli, but couldn't do it. Rude isn't something I do well and, frankly, I didn't think that was what Zane really had in mind. I had to let go and be free to do bad things.

Touching the Trees

So while I was eating with my right hand, I wrong-handedly scrawled ideas into my notebook. And before the butter could even congeal in the bottom of the empty noodle bowl, I had a list of two whole bad things to do that day that weren't too rude or too illegal. One was slightly butter-stained ("Don't actually watch *Braveheart*") and the other one ("Don't use turn signals") was illegible and already accomplished, but it was a start. Time to think a little harder.

Since I'd already pulled off the great turn signal rebellion, my Thursday bad thing was going to be to call my kid's school and complain about the ironically-named Success class. You might be thinking, "She's sticking up for her kid. That's great personal growth toward self-actualization," or something like that. But if you're me, a former middle school teacher, it feels like a bad thing to complain to a school. Even when your kid is a failure in Success class for turning in cream puff assignments late.

But before I could commit to that (I worried it might have elements of conflict that I needed to process a little more), I wanted to go home and organize the rest of my bad things. I certainly didn't want to go off half-cocked on my first mini-assignment without a clear plan for the rest of the week. But it wasn't procrastination. Honest.

At home, I sat at my desk and worked on the list. All right, I thought. "C'mon, bad things. What are you? Talk to me!" I braided my hair, surreptitiously rubbed crumbs off my cheeks, and stepped outside to have a cigarette. The next worst bad thing I could come up with on my own was carbo-loading on period day (which I was well on my way to completing, obviously), so instead of writing down more things like, "Don't do the dishes," or "Leave the garbage cans out all day," I called in professional help. Not Zane (since he'd caused this problem to begin with), but the next best thing…my sister.

My sister knows bad things. Well, not anymore because she's respectable and a professional. But she can conjure up stuff when necessary. Her two suggestions were: have a biker sign my breast and moon a school bus. Hmm. Those were…doable. Now I only needed three more baddies and I could be officially ready to start my assignment.

At that moment, my bad thing list looked like this:

- Thursday—no turn signals (again?) and yell at school
- Friday?
- Saturday?
- Sunday—have biker sign breast (Coincidentally, I was going to a biker's book signing. How fortunate for me!)
- Monday—moon school bus
- Tuesday?

As my mind waded deeper into the baby pool of my bad self, I developed some ideas for Friday. I could rat out my cousin-in-law to his soon-to-be ex-wife. After all, I'd witnessed the cousin looking all smarmy with his "alcoholic, chain-smoking, fat, ugly girlfriend" (his wife's words, not mine) on a night he was supposed to have visitation with his kids but was "sick." That would be bad, right?

I could pretend to be deaf at a Vietnamese nail salon, which would be a hoot once they started filing and painting. How would I explain that I wanted a different color? How many times would I need to have them repainted because of an accidental smudge caused by wild ASL gesturing? Maybe they'd give me the universal, single-digit sign for "You are horrible and your cuticles are NOT supposed to be a snack food!"

For Saturday, the bad things started to come easily. Reminiscent of a wedding reception I attended with my kids (where the kids clinked their glasses, the couple kissed, and the kids held up scorecards) I decided to take some self-made scorecards to the local karaoke night at the bowling alley. Someone wearing a "2005 Karaoke Champion, Naperville, Illinois" shirt facing a "6.2/10" card would be bad. "My ears are bleeding!" "Sing it, Paris Hilton!" "Your fly is open!" "Your wife just left you!" The list of Bad messages was endless. I'd bring a Sharpie marker and extra paper with me to allow the creative beer juices to flow freely from brain to paper.

After karaoke, when I would be getting just the slightest case of the post-beer munchies, I would use my last paper and my Sharpie to pen this message. "Drive-Thru Speaker is Broken. Please Speak Loudly and Slowly!" I would attach it to the 24-hour McDonald's outdoor menu, then slither through a side door and sit within earshot of the front counter.

"I WANT SOME LARGE FRIES AND A COKE!!"

"GIVE ME A BIG MAC AND SOME APPLE SLICES. WITH CARAMEL!!"

"IS BREAKFAST BEING SERVED YET?"

"CAN I HAVE A TACO?"

Saturday night drunkards can say stupid things. And I would be super bad for making them do it, loudly and slowly. **

** *Disclaimer. This idea is not original. To my knowledge, it first happened in 1984 at a McDonald's in Indianapolis. I was in the decoy party that staked out the front counter, ordered one large sleeve of fries for eight people, and giggled as the employees yelled, "STOP YELLING AT ME!"*

Sunday was covered. One biker book-signing; one Sharpie to the breast. Really. I'd purchased a book just two weeks earlier written by a member of the Outlaw biker gang and co-written by my writing teacher. The book-signing was being held in a biker bar and I was going.

Monday was Moonday for me. But I wouldn't moon my own kids' bus. That would be both bad and really wrong. So, I'd have to moon someone else's kids...preferably middle-schoolers, some of whom probably needed a pick-me-up after their own failures in Success.

For this escapade, I would wear black, elastic-waisted sweatpants, easily-yanked boxers, and my husband's hat and sweatshirt. I suppose if I really thought about it, wearing my husband's clothing to commit such a bad, potentially felonious, thing wouldn't be prudent. But I was in therapy and completing an assignment, so prudence wasn't my concern anymore. I could only hope that my husband would make the most of his supervised visits with the kids after his release from the offender center, if it came to that.

Now I had to find something for Tuesday. What could I do on Tuesday to complete my assignments? And how to cram in *Braveheart*? I didn't know, so I watched Court TV. I ate some chips. I jotted notes to the Success teacher. I called the bowling alley to confirm karaoke. I placed two Sharpies in my purse, just in case one ran out. But it wasn't procrastination. Honest.

Finally, the last bad thing came to me. I needed a tattoo. A colorful, permanent testament to my success at bad.

On Tuesday, after the kids went to school, I would dig out the phone book and find myself a tattoo parlor. I'd had a swirly design picked for years, ever since I swore I'd get ink on my 40th birthday, but had chickened out...it seemed too bad at the time. Now I had a fabulous modification to that design. My ankle would sport the word "freedom" artfully, colorfully and with great swirliness, embedded into its skin. I would be able to see that bad thing every day for the rest of my life.

And for Tuesday night, instead of watching *Braveheart*, I had a final Bad idea, albeit *Braveheart*-related. I would get a can of Hormel Chili with Beans and some linked sausage wieners. I would find an old tablecloth to make a tunic and find a leather belt to hold it in place. I'd dig out flip-flops and the big meat fork we use for summer barbecuing. I would scavenge my bathroom until I found some crumbling blue eye shadow (circa 1991), and I would smear it all over one side of my face. In my costume, I would totally resemble Mel Gibson…or his truly terrifying half-sister gnome.

Minutes before my husband got home from work, I'd send the kids downstairs with a pizza, ice cream, and carte blanche to play video games and fight with each other. I would lie down on the kitchen table. I would pile the sausages on my stomach, pour the Hormel chili all over them, and stab them with the meat fork.

And when my husband came in the door, expecting to be greeted by a great, clamoring crowd of family, all he would see would be me in the last scene of *Braveheart*, my guts eviscerated, breathily mouthing the word, "Freedom." It would scare the bejeezus out of him and I would be a very bad girl for pulling such a mean-spirited prank.

So I thought about that. I worked through the plans and the permutations. I pictured the look of pride that would cross Zane's face when he heard every bad thing I was able to accomplish. I would pretend that his look didn't really say, "Please don't sue me, please don't sue me, please don't sue me…."

But that day, after I spent all that otherwise-allocated time noodling and taking great joy in how bad of a person I could be, I closed my buttery notebook, got up from my snack-laden desk, and started my afternoon carpool run. Without turn signals, of course.

I'm a little embarrassed to tell you that I accomplished almost nothing on my list. I did go to the biker book-signing and buy the movie *Braveheart*, but that was it. Don't think I didn't want to, though. I longed to be the kind of person who could pull off such a grand week of mid-life crises. Since I wasn't, I learned this instead: At the beginning of my journey, if the only steps taken outside my comfort zone were in my imagination, that was still okay.

Chapter Two
My Cousin Betsy

There are others players in this story too, besides Zane. I have an ex-husband, three children, parents, grandparents, siblings, aunts, uncles, cousins, and friends. I've got people who landed in my life only for a brief time, for a specific purpose, and I'm fortunate to have friends that, fairly soon now, could be considered lifers.

My family of origin consists of parents that have been married to each other for over 40 years (maybe even a few of those happily), a younger brother, and two younger sisters. One layer out includes two dozen first cousins and scores of other seconds, once-removeds, and all of their spouses.

Within my first cousin group there are sub-groups. There are the older cousins (that's where I am), the giant middle group, and the few stragglers—including one who is only a year older than my oldest child.

To narrow down the older cousins even more, though, there's a small but very important unit: me and my cousin Betsy.

My cousin Betsy is one of the funniest people I know. Her descriptions of her younger daughter—a curly-headed blondie with enormous innocent blue eyes—as the spawn of Satan make me cross my legs and try to hold it while I throw my head back and laugh. Her stories about her husband's various "bionic" parts—he's been in more than his share of freak accidents—always make me wish I'd gone to the girls' room fifteen minutes earlier.

But Betsy's also the reason I finally feel part of my extended family. Which is a surprise, since I was bred to hate her guts.

I was raised by a mother who has always resented her older sister. When my mom was born in 1942, she was the second of what would eventually be eight children. She was the second daughter of my grandfather (the second son) and my grandmother (the second daughter). There is significant numerology there, and she always felt nothing better than second best.

See, she was also born with a deformed hand. To this day no one knows why, but her right hand didn't grow right. She was missing two bones in her index finger and her two middle fingers were bent at 90 degree angles. Her thumb and pinkie looked almost normal, but were smaller than the ones on her left hand. I can't imagine what it must have been like for her, growing up in the 40s with that kind of impediment, but she did it all—learned to write, type, play basketball, sew, milk cows...you name it and she made it happen.

Then there was her sister Beverly. Aunt Beverly was the first-born, the one with two perfectly good hands and who was a normal height (unlike my 6-foot tall mom). She was smart, pretty, and, according to my mom, the "perfect child." She had a nice wedding to a quiet Navy officer, bore three kids, and travelled the world. It wasn't until Aunt Beverly divorced that quiet Navy officer 30 years later that my mom felt she had the upper hand. Bev's divorce wasn't the first in the family, but she was *Beverly*. And my mom, who maybe should have divorced my dad years and years ago, probably never will even though she beat Beverly in the marriage-longevity contest.

I was the oldest child in my family and the first granddaughter. My cousin Betsy was the second child in her family, the second granddaughter, and only about six months younger than me. We were supposed to become great cousin-friends and were always thrown together at reunions. Granted, we had some fun times (I will forever have a soft spot for the song "When the Lights Went Out in Georgia" thanks to an awesome dance/lip syncing routine we created somewhere around 1974), but we drifted apart once we hit middle school age and her dad was stationed in Hawaii for four years.

Around this time I decided to dislike Betsy. I'm embarrassed to say that I did this solely for my mother's benefit. She seemed to hate Aunt Beverly, so the least I could do to win my mom's favor was to dislike Aunt Beverly's daughter. There wasn't anything overt—after all, we hardly saw each other during the whole time I felt that way—and it wasn't something I constantly thought about. But I believed that I could please my mom by feeling that way.

Years went by; Betsy and I both got married, became adults (maybe not in that backwards order for her, but certainly for me), and had our children.

Then came our cousin Ciara's wedding. Ciara's wedding was held in a little town outside Cincinnati, Ohio, and the first trip in a long, long time that I didn't have my kids with me. At one point during the reception, I snuck outside to have a cigarette. Shortly after that, my cousin Betsy came out too. We chatted, we smoked, and we joked about hiding from our parents even though we were in our late 30s at the time.

Then she said something that changed me forever.

Sitting on that cement curb outside the reception hall, me in my green linen pants with no panties (in my defense, I was trying to avoid panty lines—had I known then what I know now about Betsy's sense of humor, I definitely would have worn a cotton liner at the very least) and Betsy in a long skirt, we started talking.

Betsy told me about how she'd always felt sorry for me because of my dad. She said she'd had long talks with my grandma about how my mom wouldn't stand up for me and how he controlled me so tightly. She said they'd talked about how sad they were that I didn't get to have as carefree a childhood and young adulthood as I deserved. She wondered, gently, how my marriage was working out since there seemed to be some control issues there, too. In short, we bonded.

Maybe this wasn't her conscious intention, but that little window of conversation showed me that I wasn't alone—that someone in that great big family, one that I valued so much but had felt apart from for so long, cared about me and had been watching out all this time. It was an amazing moment. My cousin Betsy, my nemesis-by-proxy, reached out to tell me that they still loved me and always had.

I've carried that nugget around ever since and have reached for it when my world's felt crumbly. I was raised with conditional love. I married into conditional love. I believed that there must be something called love that didn't have strings attached, but I'd never felt it nor witnessed it growing up. The first time I'd felt unconditional anything was when I had my own children and vowed they'd never need to prove themselves worthy. But my cousin Betsy showed me that there was unconditional love out there. And it was within my own family.

So I bypassed my mother and all of her resentful baggage and became friends with Betsy starting that very night. At our hotel we sat outside, drinking beer and laughing through childhood memories with a couple of other cousins and their spouses. The act of defying my mom's unspoken wishes was no small feat, however. My parents always kept us kids a little separated from the rest of the herd. We were told we were smarter, more talented, and most likely to succeed. To continue to reach out to Betsy meant that I had to understand that none of what my parents wanted me to believe was true. Or, more correctly, that none of it mattered. And that's exactly what I did, even as the curtains in my mom's hotel window fluttered open and shut on our little sidewalk party.

We still don't see each other very often, but I recently drove all night to be at Cousin Ciara's baby shower and to sneak smokes behind my grandma's barn with Betsy, her husband, her brother, his wife, and my sister. And I have to tell you, that woman can make a story about middle-aged daytime sex on a bathroom counter while wearing nothing but a face full of Noxzema funny. Really, really funny. Pants-peeing funny.

So it's a good thing I re-converted to wearing panties with dress pants (welcome back, panty lines) when we all met up at our cousin Amanda's wedding. I definitely needed some absorbency...

Touching the Trees

Chapter Three
Old Ladies

    Zane, the greatest therapist in the world, didn't get that title by sitting there and waiting for me to pour forth with all my inner demons, by the way. There were days when he had to use his considerable training and natural skills to coax me into conversation, which then usually led to reflection and, finally, to understanding of whatever issue I was having at the time.

    But beyond encouraging all the light bulbs that clicked on above my head during sessions, what Zane best taught me to do when I was sitting on his leathery loveseat was to trust. I learned to trust my intuition, my emotions, and my thoughts. I learned to trust that I wouldn't "fail" therapy if I took a detoured path through assignments.

It is not an overstatement to say that he was the first man in a very long time that I could trust. And that trust didn't come easily.

I first met Zane many years ago when my husband and I were in therapy for the umpty-umpth time. We met with him for a few sessions until I realized that couples therapy wasn't going to accomplish what I'd hoped it would—the creation of a happier, more fulfilling marriage in which my husband would be respectful of me and attracted to me.

Instead, my last take-away from our final session was that no one, including that dumb therapist and my idiot husband, would ever understand me. It was a low point among low points.

Then I hit rock bottom, decided to divorce my husband, and turned in desperation to the only person I knew in the counseling field—Zane. Little by little he brought me back to myself and to a place where I could trust him again.

Which is why I felt fairly confident one day (with just a hint of nerves) when I chose to skip writing my own obituary and think about my grandmas instead.

I was sitting in Zane's office one Wednesday and he asked me an uncomfortable question. Of course, it was his business to ask uncomfortable questions but this one bothered me a lot. He asked, "If you were to write your own obituary, what would you write?"

I knew what he was trying to do. I'd spent the previous session floundering in my resolve to seek out, define, and give birth to a new self. I was poised on the threshold of shucking off the housewife box I'd been in and soaring free, but was hesitant and wondering if taking a few steps backward toward the safety of an intact family wasn't a better option after all. He was trying to get me to focus on the future and all the fabulous opportunities and accomplishments within my grasp...if I would just believe in them.

What he wanted to know—or better yet, what he wanted ME to know—was what kind of life did I want to leave behind?

I refused to answer. It was too macabre, too scary and too awful to think about dying. I didn't feel like I'd quite started to live and I certainly didn't want to focus on being gone. So I turned it around. "I won't do that," I said after a long slow drink of my diet soda. "But I will tell you what kind of old lady I want to be." He raised his eyebrows and sat back into his chair without saying anything else.

I want to be an old lady like my grandmothers, I told him. My one grandmother, Grandma G, the clear matriarch of her large family of eight children, twenty-four grandchildren, and twenty-one great-grandchildren, is a widow and has been for nearly forty years. She's owned and sold a business, owned her own house and taken care of it, raised her children to be compassionate and successful, and become a master gardener. She also has a killer sweet pickle recipe that's being passed down to my generation, finally. It's from her that I got my love of gardening−preparing, planting, growing, pruning, mulching, and reaping.

But beyond all that, since I've known her, my grandmother hasn't been afraid to speak her mind. All of us grandchildren know that if you want someone's honest opinion about a topic, ask Grandma. She'll tell you. It may not be what you want to hear, but she'll tell you anyway. And if something needs talked about, she makes sure it happens.

I announced my divorce in the month of July. In late August I saw Grandma G at my parents' house. The elephant in the room, the one that no one was mentioning because I wasn't bringing it up, was that news. Then out of nowhere, during a lull in the conversation, my Grandma jumped in. "I have to tell you, I was shocked at your news."

"I know, Grandma."

"I didn't see it coming."

"I know, Grandma."

"Are you and the kids okay?"

"Yes."

"It takes a lot to surprise someone my age, but you did it. So what happened?"

"Um, we grew apart."

I knew she didn't completely buy my answer, but from that opening stemmed many questions from two aunts that were there, as well as a few from my mother (from whom I'd withheld almost all information) and so my grandmother didn't need to ask any more. But she didn't disapprove, that much I knew.

From her I learned that I wanted to be an old lady that lets no sleeping elephants lie. Ask questions, listen carefully. Tell the truth. Don't be bossy, but be firm. Never get closed-minded, but be secure in your beliefs. Be caring and capable. Surround yourself with family and friends. Volunteer to be the hub of all activity. If you love, you will be loved in return.

My grandmother never has to beg her children or grandchildren to visit. Everyone just wants to. In fact, once I drove all night from Minnesota to Ohio for just that. Like so many others in my big family, I needed to be in my grandmother's house, even for a short visit, to center myself.

My other grandmother, Grandma H, was a very different woman from that, but I felt an affinity for her because of her unassuming, quiet strength. This grandmother divorced my grandfather when she was sixty. She packed up, left him and spent a few days with my parents (who had just brought home their first newborn—me). I don't know the exact sequence of events that followed, but I know she moved into her own apartment shortly after that. I also don't know why my grandparents divorced except what my mom told me—my grandfather was a "philanderer" and my grandmother was not into physical affection.

(To this day, I remember how much my grandfather loved and spoiled me. It's because of him and his second wife Martha that I started to like orange circus peanuts. I was his clear favorite, the granddaughter he'd always wanted, and the day he died was, honestly, the last time I felt like someone's favorite for a long, long time. And I was twelve. So, he may have been a philanderer and my grandmother obviously had some good reason to divorce him, but I still miss him anyway.)

What I realized as I got older and less happy in my own marriage was this: my grandmother had a great deal of courage to leave her husband of thirty years, in 1966, and start her life over. She was a professional musician, so she was self-sufficient and financially secure. She smoked exactly one cigarette each day and rarely drank. She brought oyster stuffing to every Thanksgiving and introduced me to Brussels sprouts, which I love even now. Because of her belief in my musical talent, I played violin and piano for years.

She was a visual artist after she retired from being in the symphony and painted prolifically; her favorite medium was watercolor. I have a handful of her paintings in my house, my siblings have a few each, and my father is hoarding the rest until he downsizes beyond his ability to store them.

My grandmothers did what I hope to do—they built full lives around their families and their passions.

They didn't have to worry about subjugating themselves to their marriages. In fact, they both survived and flourished after their husbands were gone. Neither dated once they were single, but maybe that was a product of the situations and the times—Grandma G was in her mid-fifties when my grandfather died and had several children still at home, as well as a business she needed to learn and run. Grandma H was sixty and may have felt like she was too old. But they showed me that it's okay to go it alone. It can be good. It can be better.

So I sat there that one Wednesday, on Zane's loveseat, staring out the window at a field of wild grass and, beyond that, a busy gas station. I pictured myself an old lady full of wisdom and strength. I pictured myself free from the situation I was in at the time—trapped in a role I didn't want to play anymore, suffocating slowly but surely for the sake of appearances.

I pictured my children loving me despite my choice to break up our family. In fact, I pictured them loving me because of it. I pictured my grandchildren admiring me as much as I admire my own grandmothers—and not because I would demand it, but because I earned it. I pictured being a successful, retired artist. I pictured myself happy. Old and wrinkled, of course, but happy. Happier than I would be if I chose safety and security over a canyon of hope and uncertainty.

In that image of myself as an old lady, I finally saw what Zane wanted me to see—the me I'd always, always yearned to be. And the me I hoped I *could* be.

Touching the Trees

Chapter Four
Labels and Boxes
(and Some Wrapping Paper)

Speaking of husbands, I had one once. In fact, I had one for a long time, once.

Part of this story includes a twenty-year marriage to a man I met in Junior High School. He was a boy then, of course, but later he got taller than me, began shaving, became my boyfriend, and eventually vowed to be my husband.

There are days when I can't stand that guy now.

Our marriage started out just fine. We were frighteningly young (okay, we were both 22, but that seems frighteningly young *now*) and we both had decent entry-level jobs. Within a year of our marriage I quit my job to go to graduate school to become the English teacher I'd always wanted to be.

Within a few years of that, he went to graduate school to become the MBA he'd always wanted to be. During that time we also moved around and talked about starting a family.

Then with one pink plus sign and a cross-country moving van in the middle of summer, I lost being the English teacher and became someone I didn't know how to be—a stay-home parent.

I love my children; there's no question about that. And like everyone else, I entered the parenting world blind. But I had a difficult time adjusting to being alone with two very closely-spaced babies (as my husband completed his MBA and worked 70-hour weeks), being physically exhausted, and feeling like I was under the scrutiny of every other stay-home parent I knew. There seemed to be rules and expectations around being a stay-home that I wasn't sure I understood. And the ones I did understand, I wasn't sure I could meet.

So I just wasn't at all confident in my ability to fit into that role, even though I looked the part.

I know people who are precise in their wrapping. The find just the right sized box or, if they can't, they err on the side of a box that's too big and they add filler. These same people tape all the seams so that nothing can slip out. When they're applying the wrapping paper, every crease is carefully pressed; every flap is pointy and comes right to the center of the box. The label is written out, in cursive, with a specific "To" and a specific "From." That well-mannered label is affixed to the top left corner of the box, along with a loopy bow. And at the end of the process, these wrappers take great pride and pleasure in the fact that there's no question what the package is. Anyone looking at the box can tell it's a gift.

I don't wrap like that. In addition to coming from a family of women who buy cheap shoes and who can't get a birthday card in the mail earlier than three weeks late, I come from a line of present-wrappers that are inept at making a package look like something that contains anything of value. A box from me could contain diamonds and still look like it was wrapped by feet. In fact, it's often hard to tell at my family Christmases what's a present and what's just a pile of used wrapping paper.

My gifts to people, if they aren't shoved in a recycled decorative gift bag with crumpled tissue paper, resemble a crude preschool approximation of a present. If I haven't cut the right amount of paper, I've cut too little and a slice of box shows on the bottom side. When that's the case, I've been known to cut a two-inch wide addition and tape it on. The two ends of my wrapped boxes are never cornered the same—I will never understand how I can press one pair of creases one way, turn the box around, and press the other pair of creases completely differently.

Sometimes I cut too much paper, though, and my flaps are bulbous and fist-like and I'm forced to either cut them off or apply extra tape to hold them down.

Long ago I gave up labels, preferring to hunt down a permanent marker or crayon, if it's handier, and scribble who it's to and who it's from on any side that's tapeless, if there is one. Usually I add the flair of either a smiley face or a heart, mostly to make myself feel better about the lousy wrap job.

But sadly, and I hate to say this, it makes a difference—even to me, who is terrible at it—how a present is wrapped. Of course I know it *shouldn't* matter. Is the measure of a gift's worth really in how it's presented? Is it what's on the outside that's important, or what's on the inside? And haven't we been taught that about people, too? "Beauty is in the eye of the beholder." "Don't judge a book by its cover." So what does it mean when the box reflects on the gift?

So I got to thinking about boxes, labels, wrappings and relationships. One of my biggest struggles in my marriage was feeling boxed in. At the time it was certainly more of an emotional sense of enclosure, but I'd also gone through many years of feeling physically boxed in. When my kids were younger, the walls of the house would close in on me if we couldn't go somewhere, even if it was to the dreaded grocery store. But we couldn't always leave the house—if one child was sick, or the effort was too great, or if I didn't feel like showering for the second day in a row, we'd stay in and I'd feel stuck.

Feeling emotionally boxed in by my marriage was a different, more insidious sensation not completely unlike being fake-eviscerated on the kitchen table. I didn't feel free to express "negative" emotions, like anger or sadness or frustration. I swallowed my feelings every day, along with an anti-depressant and sometimes a few ibuprofens.

I can see now that I created that box, to some extent, by allowing my fear of rejection or reprisal control how I thought and felt. But I also played the relationship game, acted out my role, and reaped the rewards—cars, trips, and a lake house—that were supposed to make my world so much happier. That box, if I'd dared to use a permanent marker to write on my forehead, would have been labeled, "Wife."

The wife box I was in was wrapped in yellowed, soggy fairy tale. The seams came unglued little by little over the years and the lid had difficulty staying closed. During various conciliation periods I stuck all kinds of tape on it to hold it together—patience tape, forgiveness tape, martyr tape, therapy tape, and kid tape—but in the end, there wasn't enough adhesive in the world to keep that box from disintegrating. It just plain fell apart. So I stepped over the wreckage, and quit being a wife.

But there's a problem with turning your back on the rubble of a twenty-year identity. It's not easy to float around in your life and not have someone, somewhere, want to put you back in a box, including (unfortunately) yourself. Those same people who wrap neatly and precisely? They sometimes feel a tremendous need to have everything in its place, labeled so that it's understood. And me, the one who doesn't put much stock in bows or matching up vertical stripes? Even I've been tempted to find a new box to crawl into because it's scary to be so exposed. It's also easier to know who you are when your expectations and behaviors are defined by four sides, a bottom, and a top—even if the box doesn't fit quite right and you have to add some filler in the form of fake smiles and mom jeans.

Now that I've finalized my divorce, settled into a pattern of raising my kids on my own and considered dating, I've had a hard time explaining to friends and family why my heels are dug in and my arms are stretched across the doorframes of the boxes they want me to step into. Really, those boxes are easier. They are scripted. They are structured and make sense to everyone. Inside the divorcee box is a person who is on the hunt for a husband and who is frazzled with fear and responsibility. Her box looks suspiciously like the wife box, but with far fewer power tools and televisions.

Inside the single parent box is the woman who would rather be on dates than with the kids and who is steeling herself for them to fall apart in some colossal fashion. Or maybe she's decided to put every ounce of her energy into being a supermom, at the expense of herself. Either way, that box is wrapped in grocery bags and held together with poison-control stickers and PTA announcements.

Inside the new girlfriend box is a person who devotes her life to being half of a couple and who puts everything that doesn't fit in the new girlfriend box out on the curb for pickup including, sometimes, the kids. That package is wrapped in trendy, fashionable paper and everyone knows that being inside the new girlfriend box means you are again a person of value.

And I reject all of them, despite the fact that the new girlfriend box, with its beautiful grass-is-greener paper (and possibly some new lingerie), is awfully inviting.

Unlike some other new divorcees I've met, I'm not going to go bar-hunting and sling one-night-stands all over the city only to have my self-esteem (and possibly my cheap shoes) lost in the process. Unlike some single parents I know, I'm not going to resent alone time with my children. Instead, I'm going celebrate their incredible resilience and relish the fact that I can holler at them to get their homework done without worrying about losing their love.

All of which is great for me and my search for identity, but it doesn't really solve the problem of labels and boxes. Even if we can create and live in a world without manuals of defined behavior for each of our relationships, that doesn't mean some of the people around us can. Even if we believe that everything will be okay and that we'll never have the pinched look of a person picking through garbage for a new box, that doesn't mean other people won't perceive our laugh lines as wrinkles of bitterness and dissatisfaction.

We can't help what other people do or what they believe. For years and for their sakes, all of us have at times wrapped ourselves in pink heart-and-roses paper, or paper with bold, rebellious shades of blue, or even paper that has subtle, meek undertones of a pastel, Easter-egg yellow. We've done that so those other people would think they knew us…and so we could try to know ourselves.

We can learn this, though, even if we aren't ready to jump into a new identity: Underneath all that wrapping may be a box. But in that box is a person—you, me, a friend, or a neighbor. And each of us is a gift anyway.

Chapter Five
Diamond Rings and Padded Bras

When I was a young girl, my mom hated Barbie. She hated the whole idea of Barbie: the sexiness, the flirtatiousness, the materialism and the emphasis on social stature. She hated Barbie so much that she vowed to never get us one and made it clear to extended family that neither my sisters nor I were to ever receive one as a gift.

Then my friend Mitzy came to my 10th birthday party. Apparently Mitzy didn't get the memo, because in her package to me was a beautiful, blonde Barbie. I loved that doll.

But as right as that gift seemed, my joy was tempered by the fact that my mom didn't like it at all.

I remember other gifts that didn't quite work. There was the board game for a child much younger than me (it also had a missing piece because of its garage sale origin) from my step-grandmother. There were the two pepper shakers my parents got me from a trip. (It was actually my friend Kat that collected salt and pepper shakers…*salt* and pepper shakers, not me. I collected pigs.)

But to prove that I'm not ungrateful, because I'm really not, I was ecstatic to receive some beautifully spot-on gifts like some orange espadrilles from my parents when I was ten, a kitten from my new husband when I turned 23 and a kick-butt camera when I reached 40.

To also prove that I'm nowhere close to perfect in all things gift-related, I am not only a terrible present wrapper, but a terrible gift giver as well. One prime example—for our first anniversary I gave my husband a pewter figurine of a golfer astride an amethyst quartz, teeing up a crystal ball. It was crip-a-crap. And it showed how little I understood him and what he might want.

Kitten and camera notwithstanding, he wasn't so good at understanding what I wanted either, though.

"Men only give you what they give you…when they know they can't give you what you want." Catherine, in Robert Goolrick's *The Reliable Wife*, lamented that her husband gave her baubles—jewelry, silver, silk, and china—in place of what she really wanted. The problem, in her case, was that she didn't know exactly what it was that she wanted. She just knew that it wasn't those symbols of wealth and status. It was something deeper and more vital. Something like love with a measure of stability thrown in.

  I can trace back over twenty years and point out every time I was given something from my husband that was supposed to stand in, like a proxy, for what I really needed. And I knew what I needed. I needed to be cherished. I needed the comfort of human touch. I needed to trust. I needed to love and to know that I was loved in return.

  Instead I got baubles. Worse, I got a whole lot of effort spent on trying to convince me that my needs were merely wants—and that wants were not only optional, but often selfish. According to my husband, wants were like pipedreams. They were not necessary for survival; they merely caused temporary happiness. All those things I supposedly needed? He didn't believe they were necessary for me because he didn't believe they were necessary for him.

  I remember the time he came home from a business trip in another state. He came in the door, took one look at me, and went upstairs to the bathroom. I followed him to see if he was sick, and he was. But he didn't have the flu. He was sick because he had some really awful news to tell me.

He'd had a one-night stand at his hotel just two nights before. He was sick with disappointment in himself and, I suppose, with fear about what he'd done to me and to our marriage.

I'd assumed our marriage was strong. I'd assumed that affairs only happened to other people. I assumed that I would walk out immediately, like everyone always says they will when confronted with the same situation. I also assumed that he would try to make it up to me if I stayed. And he tried, but not in the ways I needed him to.

Shortly after he confessed this and many other transgressions he'd been hiding, we went on a pre-planned trip back to see our families. On the way there, I fell asleep in the car, far too emotionally exhausted to fight through the lull of the road.

When we got close to our destination, I woke up to find him staring at me. "You looked so peaceful while you were asleep that I almost pulled over so I could kiss you," he said. "But I didn't want to wake you up and figured you probably wanted to get there before it got too late."

Granted, I needed the sleep, but I needed that kiss and the promise of new fidelity even more.

A couple of months later, at Christmas, I was still waiting for him to re-commit to me and our relationship. On television, couples in our kind of crisis went on long-coveted trips together. They went on retreats or cruises so they could rebuild trust. This was no television show, but I needed to see that I was still important to him and that he would do anything to keep us together.

On Christmas morning, I had three presents under the tree from him. After I unwrapped them, they were revealed to be: a set of salt and pepper shakers, a tin of flavored popcorn, and two potholders. He said, "I didn't want you to think I was buying back your love." He was absolutely right that I didn't want him to buy me. But I needed so much more than the hedged bet I felt in those cheap, mundane gifts.

A few years after that, when my first son was under three months old, I loved feeling his soft baby hand caressing my back as he nursed and his head snuggled in close while he napped on my chest. And I loved rubbing his legs and his round belly and his fuzzy hair. He and I touched quite a bit in those days because I was in continual awe of the creation that was my child.

Then one day I realized how much I craved that physical connection. I realized that the ache I felt when I saw my husband hug someone else or extend a pat on the back or a handshake was the unfulfilled wish that it would be me he was touching. I also realized that I was getting my need met by a baby because my own husband wouldn't touch me unless he wanted to have sex. So I pointed that out to him.

"It makes me sad that I get more physical contact with my child than I do with you."

He replied, "I just don't need it as much as you do. You probably need it too much, but I'm glad you can get it somewhere."

After my second son was born, my husband took a big job in a new city. I didn't want to move but his career seemed to demand it, so we bought a giant house with more room than we needed so that I could have visitors come and stay with me for extended periods of time. That year I needed roots, though, an extended network of friends to support me as a mother, and the ease of navigating around a city I already knew. I needed to know that he could pick my needs over his own. I got a large concrete foundation instead.

Much later, when we were preparing for the birth of our third child, we discussed the potential of having more children. I felt sure that I didn't want any more kids and he agreed wholeheartedly. So I asked him if he would get a vasectomy. After all, I argued, I'd taken birth control pills for years and years. I'd given birth and was about to give birth again. I'd lost my figure and was ravaged with stretch marks and dark circles under my eyes. I needed him to do this one thing—to take the burden of having surgery right after having my last baby off of me. I needed to know that he cared enough about our family to ease my load, just a little.

Instead: "No one is going anywhere near my 'junk'. I'm afraid of needles. Especially ones that get that close to my parts." In a prophetic twist, he also said, "I knew a guy that got divorced because he wouldn't get a vasectomy. His wife thought he was being selfish. I'm just telling you it's not for me."

So I had my tubes tied. But they apparently came untied and I got pregnant again less than a year later. On the way to the hospital a month after that surprising news, great clots of blood coming out of me, my heart palpitating, and my hands almost completely numb, I called him on a cell phone from my friend's car and told him something was really, really wrong. I needed him to go home to relieve the friend who was taking care of the kids or to come to the hospital to relieve the one that was driving me there. He said, "I'm heading into a meeting right now. Have someone call me when you know more about what's going on. You've got her there and someone else watching the kids, right? You don't need me." Oh, but I did.

What I thought was a miscarriage was an exploded ectopic pregnancy. What I thought was sleepiness was semi-consciousness brought on by a dangerous, plunging blood pressure. He finally made it there in time for the emergency surgery.

That Christmas, he bought me a diamond ring of my choosing. It was the size of Texas. My rationale for picking it? I would try to speak his language of money and things. I would try to need material trinkets rather than emotional security. I would make myself believe that he wouldn't have bought it if he didn't love me.

The funny thing is, though, that beautiful ring didn't make me feel any better than those three little gifts from years before.

After I came slothfully slow to the realization that he may have never loved me in any meaningful way, I asked him for the divorce. I needed to be free to grow as a person, I told him. I needed to be apart from him to see if I would miss him, I said. I needed to make decisions for myself, live on my own, and experience the world as a whole individual—not as the less consequential half of our marriage partnership.

"That's not what you need," he shot back in anger one night. "You need me to pay attention to you, take you away on trips, to spend more time with the kids, to buy you a new car, to support your weight loss, to desire you, and to value your parenting skills and your passion for writing."

Okay, he had some of those right.

"You also need more time with me, not less. You need me to check up on you, shorten your leash, and save you from yourself. You're a narcissist and a saboteur who can't stand to be happy and you need oversight and consequences. You need me to take care of you because you can't take care of yourself."

In the last eighteen months of our marriage, he bought me that new car. He also bought me bras and panties from Victoria's Secret (three matching sets, none that fit right), a trip to a resort in winter, a trip to Florida in summer, shoes, shirts, boots, earrings, necklaces, books, a laptop computer, and family vacations to South Dakota, Colorado, and Puerto Rico. He took me to nice restaurants and in-town getaways. He gave me baubles when I needed a breath. Like the padded bras that were a cup size too big, his version of my needs didn't fit me either.

At one point during that time, he allowed me to go away for three weekends to work on my novel, as long as I didn't characterize it as a trial separation to myself or anyone else—but checked in with me every few hours. He came over for a "date" late one night, argued with me until three in the morning another night, and minimized the amount of time I had to write by forcing me to pay attention to his texts and calls.

I needed freedom from him and his oppression and manipulation. I needed to feel joy at my own accomplishment. I needed to be able to look myself in the eye and know that I was living as fully and authentically as possible. I needed to be non-dependent on him. I needed to think clearly and make decisions based on my own knowledge.

I needed to be away from him…but he wanted me to stay. So for a time he convinced me that his want was more important than my need, since I wasn't even smart enough to know what I was searching for wasn't a need, according to him. Mine was a want, just like his, he said. Only my want was wrong.

This shell game of him trying to define for me what it was that I needed continued all the way through the divorce process and even into the post-divorce period. He said, "You needed to be independent, so why am I supposed to financially support you once we're divorced?" "You needed a break from the kids, so why shouldn't I take 50% custody?" "You never liked material things, so why should you get half of the personal property?" He turned every one of my needs back on itself and used it against me during negotiations. Even months after the divorce, he claimed that my need to be with friends was ridiculously petty if it impeded his opportunities to hang out with those same people. He decided he should get first right of refusal, since, again, my need was just a want. And my want was selfish since it was at odds with his own.

I still have that super-sized diamond ring. It's in a jeweler's box in my sock drawer. It sits there, tainted, because its beauty doesn't outweigh the loveless reasons it rode around on my finger. I also still have those pretty bras with the padded cups and rhinestones that I'll never wear. I also have some sandals he bought me for a vacation and a shirt (almost identical to one I already owned) that he bought me for our last Christmas together. I have all those things he thought I should want.

But now that I'm free of him, I may finally get what I need.

There have been times since the divorce that I've heard my ex-husband's voice in my head saying, "Be careful what you ask for." And he's got a valid point. I asked for independence and authenticity. What accompanied those two things, unfortunately, were financial insecurity and an unstable future. This "real" life I'm leading now is sometimes scary and often nerve-wracking.

My apologies for the lengthy, detailed account of the very worst of my marriage, but I shared it for a reason: None of us are alone in our pain and frustrations. We all have needs that aren't being met and shame in how we've behaved because of that. But we can learn how to make our lives work better *anyway*.

We can look back and say, "Yes, that's who I was and that's what I allowed in my life."

Then we can also say, "No more."

If someone's giving us what we don't need, guess what? We really don't need it.

Touching the Trees

Chapter Six
Touching the Trees, Part 1

The part of this story that has consumed me for the better part of many years is my relationship with and identity because of my former husband.

He was my friend in middle and high school. He was a partner in geek; we shared many classes together and had a weird competitive grades thing going. I can still, to this day, tell you what we both scored on the SAT (I beat him by a mere 20 points…on *math* of all things).

I knew him as a well-dressed military kid. He knew me as a musically-inclined suburban kid. We dated around each other during those years—he and my brother dated some of the same girls; I dated just about everyone else in our nerd herd.

We went to college hundreds of miles away from each other and didn't begin corresponding until close to our freshman year Christmas break.

Then the bottom fell out of our newly free, nearly grownup world.

Our best friend died.

After the shock, after the funeral and after we returned to our respective universities, we began writing to each other in earnest. He was the only one who understood how I felt about facing, full-on, our mortality, and I was that same person for him.

By the following summer, we were hanging out together. Eventually that hanging out was dating. Eventually that dating was something more and before we knew it, we were making plans to visit a clinic. It changed our lives forever.

I know now that one of the reasons I married him was to escape from my parents. I know one of the reasons he married me was to escape from his guilt. I also know that I loved him in the best ways I knew how for as long as I could. There are days when I believe he did the same thing.

But it had to end. The marriage and I weren't able to co-exist once I finally allowed myself to understand that I didn't want to be his wife anymore. I couldn't force it—the role I'd played for so long had clouded beyond recognition. So I said goodbye.

Luckily, my family had a history of goodbye.

My great-great-grandfather's name was Strangeman Harper. From what I've been told, and it hasn't been a whole lot, he was a Quaker minister who lived in Virginia. Since one of the main tenets of the Quaker faith is a one-on-one relationship with God, Quaker ministers were nice to have, but not necessarily essential. So he was also a farmer.

According to my grandmother (Strangeman's granddaughter), at some point in their lives Strangeman Harper and his wife, Elizabeth, were forced to leave their land. The only story my grandmother knew about that time was this:

Elizabeth was heartbroken to leave her homestead. On her last day there, after all the packing and loading was completed, she walked through the woods surrounding their land and touched all the trees. I can almost picture her using the fingertips of both hands to commit to memory how one tree's bark differed from another. I can nearly hear her whisper, "Take care, old one," as she passed by the gnarled kings and queens least likely to survive another winter.

I'm sure she believed that her one-on-relationship with God gave her strength to move forward. But she had to say goodbye to her life on that land in the best way she knew how.

Touching the Trees

I didn't hear that story until my own grandmother was nearing the end of her life. I'd asked her questions about her childhood, her earliest memories, her musical career and highlights. But this is the story she most wanted to tell me; the one she wanted me to remember. Touch the trees.

During my grandmother's easy-chair telling, it was easy to feel Elizabeth's anguish. I could feel the bark under my own fingers, maybe oak or maybe maple, each tree unique—each tree there long before her time and each tree there, serving as a witness to her life, after she left.

At the time my grandmother told me this story, I was living in the same city as her and the rest of my family, in a brand-new house. My new husband and I had saved $1500, which seemed like a fortune at the time, by painting the entire interior ourselves, including caulking, finishing the door frames, and putting three coats (one of primer, two of paint) on every square inch of wall. We poured our time, weekends and weekends of it, into getting that house ready to move into. We recruited friends and family, ordered pizza after pizza, and picked paint speckles off of our forearms at work every Monday. When the time came to haul our few things from the apartment to the new house, it felt like home.

Eighteen months after moving into that dream house—at 1,532 square feet of slab, partially carpeted in forest green, and boasting pink countertops—we had to move because of his first job transfer. On our last day—

after I'd quit my job teaching as the English department chair at a brand-new middle school down the road, and after we'd said goodbye to friends and family—I watched the final load get put on the moving truck.

Standing there on the concrete driveway, looking back at the first house I'd ever owned, my grandmother's story about touching the trees washed over me. But I only had one tree on that sparse lot and that didn't seem like enough of a goodbye.

So I went into the hollow house and headed to the back closet. Starting there, I made my way through the entire house, touching every wall and every doorframe I'd spent so many hours painting and repainting. I tried to memorize the feel of my house and even laid my cheek against the crooked, over-spackled wall we never got quite right.

By the time I touched first the white inside, then the red outside of the front door as it closed behind me, I was ready. I'd said goodbye.

I've moved many times and not every move was a dramatic event. But a couple of them were. When we moved from the house we'd lived in with the kids for eight years, I had to touch the places in their closets where they'd left painted handprints. I had to touch the wall on which we'd kept track of their heights. I had to touch the lavender paint of my favorite bathroom and the brushed nickel of the basement bar sink faucet I'd splurged on. And, yes, I had to touch the frosty-berried crabapple tree that stood by the front door.

But then I was ready to move.

Three years later, when it came time to leave my marriage, I was in awe of the significance of this particular move. Yes, I was leaving the lakeside home where we'd planned to finish raising the kids. But more importantly, I was leaving behind the trees of a relationship that had once meant something to me. It was a relationship that I'd put hours and hours into creating and maintaining.

Like my great-great-grandmother, I believe it's important to touch the trees when you say goodbye.

There was a tiny window of opportunity for me to do that at the end of my marriage. On our 20th anniversary, which fell in-between when we made the final decision to divorce and when I moved out, I asked a favor of him—to just lie still. Starting at his feet, I touched nearly every part of his skin. When I got to his arms, tears rolled down his face and he whispered, "Why are you doing this?" But he knew the answer before I could say it; he'd seen me do it before.

"I'm touching your trees," I whispered back. I tried to keep from crying myself because I wanted to remember those last moments without the lens of tears. But it was fruitless. I knew I'd never touch those trees again. I'd never be back.

We've fought like mortal enemies in the time since that night. We've wanted to screw each other over, exalt our own positions, and push the other one from our thoughts. We've argued over the kids, the houses, paintings, neighbors, friends, "space" and "respect." It hasn't been easy or pleasant to extricate ourselves from the relationship we were in before. But I don't regret saying goodbye in the way that I did. Really, it was the only way I could.

Now I'm in a period of welcoming new experiences, new joy, and new people into my life. And I've been wondering if it wouldn't be good to touch the trees as they arrive, rather than waiting until the end. So I find myself reaching out, sometimes without thought. I touch photos of the kids, my piano, wine bottles, and framed pictures. I touch my new table—the first one I ever bought on my own—and the four stools that sit under it. I touch the lavender in my yard, rub the stems between my fingers, and inhale. These are the trees of my life.

I'm touching them already. I'm saying hello. And I think this is important too.

We can't always decide when to say goodbye and sometimes that choice isn't even ours to make. But we can decide to greet, welcome, accept and trust. We can decide to notice the trees of our relationships—to nurture them and cherish them.

And when the time comes to say farewell—as it inevitably will, whether it's at the end of our lives or before—we can touch those trees, finding each one through a haze of sadness, missing them more than we thought was possible, and knowing they will stand witness to the love that created them.

Touching the Trees

Part II.
Looking Up

Chapter Seven
Abortion and the Egg Farmer's Daughter

This story has included people, certainly. It's included history, mine and others'. But it also includes decisions—breath-holding, heart-breaking, excruciating and life-altering decisions.

There have been times when I've made decisions to act, like when I finally decided to uproot all that I knew and get divorced. There have been times when I've made the decision *not* to act, like when I walked away from conflict after conflict rather than fight back.

There have also been a few times when I've made the difficult decision to speak my heart when it would have been easier and safer to stay quiet.

An abiding theory of the universe says that every action causes a reaction: every droplet causes a ripple and every breath continues a life. What happens in the seconds after any event causes another chain of actions and reactions.

And sometimes what might at first seem like one type of decision ends up being something totally different.

When it comes to talking about abortion, there have generally been three rules: If you're against abortion, it's okay to talk about it in public. If you're not against abortion, you should keep that to yourself. And if you've had one, don't tell a soul.

What our society and its churches and politicians have been focused on for so many years is the actual act of the abortion—stopping a heart, ending a life, and forcibly removing an embryo or fetus from a woman's body. What is rarely talked about is what happens after the abortion, which might be the most important part of any woman's abortion story, if she dared to share it.

Talking with a woman about her abortion is akin to going through a long series of passwords, secret handshakes, and dark corridors in order to enter her most private place. No one I know who's had one has ever offered it up in sober conversation, and it's a given that once you know someone else has had one, you keep that secret for her forever. Having an abortion reshapes a woman's core, but she may never share those life lessons with anyone because she's afraid of revealing her deepest secret and being judged by society.

But silence breeds fear…

So I'd like to tell you the secret story of mine.

When I was 20 years old, I became pregnant during my Christmas break from college. I didn't realize it until after I'd traveled to California for a month and prepared to go back to campus. I remember sitting in my family doctor's office, having had my home test confirmed by a professional, and trying to breathe through the shock. It was devastating news, absolutely devastating, because I knew my parents would more than likely pull me from school and throw me out of the house. I was the oldest child, the "good" one who had to be perfect at all times. I was at an expensive school, the daughter of professionals who were known and well-regarded in the community, and my path to success had been clearly charted out. I wasn't allowed to screw up.

In reality, I was already screwing up before the pregnancy—I was floundering and unfocused in college: sleeping through classes, drinking too much beer, and pining away for my boyfriend who was in school over 600 miles away (when he wasn't home with me for unfortunately-timed Christmas breaks). This was just the final straw.

Being young, pregnant, and unmarried meant I needed to make a quick decision, so I—along with my boyfriend, who was a Catholic boy with military parents who wouldn't have handled the news well either— made that decision in secret, just the two of us. We would not have this baby.

I don't remember a lot of what happened between that day and the abortion three weeks later, except: I had two dear friends who loaned me money without asking questions; I nearly missed the train that would take me to the city where the procedure would happen; and, my boyfriend and I slept in a flea-bag motel with a communal bathroom the night before the termination.

On the actual day, I remember the doctor trying his damnedest to talk me out of it (by explaining the procedure in great and gory detail, chastising me for not taking my birth control pills correctly, and talking about possible side effects like death and sterilization) like he was reading from some state-mandated script designed to get me to change my mind or, at the very least, never darken his door again.

Then a little bit later I had the abortion, alone and without pain medication.

What happened over the next few days is the secret that many women who have had abortions don't talk about—not because we don't want to, but because it's so hard to crack the shameful silence.

I became pro-life. But not pro-life in that I was anti-abortion. Not at all—I knew then and I know now that having the abortion was the right decision for me.

I became pro-life because I realized that I could choose to make my abortion mean something. I could choose to make life better for me and those around me *because of it*.

So I did. I deliberately, with a conviction I didn't know I possessed, chose to not let that heartbeat die in vain.

Two days after the abortion, I went back to school, studied hard, raised my grades and quit drinking so much and so often. I found jobs on campus (one in a dorm kitchen and one in the library), worked whenever I wasn't in class or studying, and repaid my friends. I helped my boyfriend deal with his guilt and committed to being a better partner. I chose to move forward instead of languishing in complacency. I vowed to raise the children I would hopefully one day have as well as I possibly could, and take anything that came my way with grace and humility.

I am a better person today because of my abortion. This may lead people to think I'm a whole-sale advocate for abortion. I'm not, but neither do I judge what other women decide to do. I'm just a better person than I was and I suspect other women are, too.

However, this part of my story has been a secret for over twenty years because I believed I needed to protect myself with silence.

Until I met an egg farmer.

Last spring, with two friends, I enjoyed my first day-long St. Patrick's Day celebration. We started at a bar owned by another friend, walked ourselves to a second one to listen to the St. Paul police bagpipers, and ended up at a third one on a private patio overlooking the river. It was an uncharacteristically beautiful March 17th—the sun was shining and it was warm enough to be outside with my jacket tied around my waist instead of zipped up to my chin.

At some point on that patio, my single friend noticed two men at the bar, one who was definitely her type—tall, dark-haired, lean, and drinking white wine—and one who was not. Being the gregarious person she is and given how long we'd been bar-hopping, she started up a conversation with the dark-haired one while our other friend and I hung out with the wingman.

We opened by asking about the lanyards the guys were wearing. Their story was that they were egg farmers from Arkansas who were in St. Paul for an agricultural convention. Further ice-breaking revealed that both men were ex-cons, both had been incarcerated for crimes related to methamphetamines, and both were employed as part of a rehabilitation project.

A little later, just as nearly all possible talk about egg farming and incarceration had been exhausted, the three of us wing-people noticed that the discussion next to us had veered away from casual flirtatiousness and was headed toward stridency. Only a couple of seconds after that, we realized that the topic causing the problem was abortion.

See, my friend is a pro-choice, converted Catholic. Her egg-farmer was not so pro-choice, not so Catholic and, coincidentally, the father of a young woman who'd recently had an abortion. He told us about how his daughter got pregnant by accident, chose to have an abortion, and was riddled with guilt over that decision. He pointed to his daughter's reaction to the abortion as another reason why abortion is across-the-board wrong. He felt like if she hadn't had access to an abortion, she wouldn't be feeling so wracked by her decision.

To the egg farmer's credit, he most definitely felt compassion for his daughter's pain; we could see it in his furrowed brow and faraway stares. But what he didn't see (probably because she didn't see it yet either) was that she was stuck on the choice to have the abortion. She really needed to move away from the decision she couldn't change and take a step toward making decisions for her future.

Of course she felt guilty, but that guilt was exacerbated because she hadn't yet chosen to make her abortion mean something. *Of course* she felt sad, but that sadness was paralyzing because she hadn't yet chosen to keep that heartbeat from dying in vain. And I didn't feel like I could tell him that.

After my abortion, I chose to make significant changes in my life, just like many other women have, but it wasn't an easy road. My parents eventually found out about the abortion by reading my mail (my mother had a habit of removing letters from sealed envelopes and replacing them using a pencil-rolling technique I later made her show me) and were at least as heartless and cruel as they would have been if I'd tearfully confessed the pregnancy in the first place. "You have killed our first grandchild." "If you have sex again before marriage, you will be out of this family." "Any future husband of yours will never be able to run for political office." (The last comment was so absurd that I should have laughed, but couldn't.) I lost all faith in them as my caretakers and that faith wasn't rebuilt.

Also, I married that boyfriend as a way to prove to myself and my parents that I wasn't one of "those girls" and he married me to mitigate the enormous Catholic guilt he felt. That, too, didn't work out very well.

But I graduated with honors from college, went to graduate school on a fellowship, became the teacher I always wanted to be and then the writer I always hoped I could be. I had three children who are open-hearted, intelligent, and talented and for whom I have tried to be the best mother I could imagine. I have also worked hard to be a respectful, considerate, and giving member of my family and my community.

And all of that is so the decision made when I was still a college student—when I was the equivalent of that egg farmer's daughter—wouldn't be for nothing.

Our choices impact us and people around us, now and into the future. The enormity of that truth can be frightening because a "wrong" decision can seem to have ultimate consequences. We have the chance to make all of our decisions meaningful, though.

Even if the only thing we learned was to never make that particular choice again, it's a learning that has purpose.

Chapter Eight
Arrows, Downward and Up

There have been times in my life when I've been depressed. When I was sixteen it was so bad that I took my new license and my old Plymouth Valiant and drove myself to a therapist to seek help. At the time I was over-extended, over-achieving, and under-loved and couldn't seem to shake the desperate feeling that I didn't belong in my family. I saw nothing but a future of trying to meet increasingly difficult expectations placed on me by a father that saw me as a commodity and/or a trophy.

Touching the Trees

At the age of 23, just a few months after graduating from college, taking my first job at a public relations firm, and getting married, I found myself coming home from work at 5:30 and falling asleep on the couch until it was time to eat or go to bed. There was a several-month-long period where I could only stomach instant mashed potatoes during my brief waking times. I lost weight and interest in my job and my husband. What finally pulled me out of it then was a doctor saying there was nothing physically wrong with me and a job counselor placing in my hand an application for a grad school fellowship that I was eventually awarded.

Another bout of depression came on when I was 30. I had a 20-month old, an 8-month old, had moved across the Midwest just three months before for my husband's job. I was so foggy and exhausted that I could barely function. I went to the doctor thinking that my thyroid was acting up, since I'd had trouble with it in the past. But on my 31st birthday, I had a phone message from the doc saying that my thyroid was okay, but she was diagnosing me with depression. She prescribed an anti-depressant that I started taking that very day.

I remember feeling devastated, though. I remember feeling like: If I wasn't depressed enough already, getting a message on my birthday telling me I was might just be enough to send me over the edge. But the meds eventually worked and I felt better.

Fast forward eleven years… I was still a housewife, still a stay-home mother, had moved two more times, and was heading toward another depression. I'd also lost a great deal of weight (on purpose this time), been unable to re-spark my husband's interest in me, and started wondering how many more bottles of anti-depressants I'd need to stay married.

Here I was: a woman who'd battled depression for over 25 years, who couldn't visualize a future without the husband I'd come to fear, who didn't feel like I had one ounce of courage or energy, and who was blind to any positives about myself. I needed help and I needed it desperately.

Fortunately, I was already seeing Zane again and had built up enough trust in him to believe that he might be able to provide some relief from my anguish. Each of Zane's assignments and exercises prior to this low point were helpful in one way or another, but there was one that changed my life forever.

It was called the Downward Arrow.

The gist of the Downward Arrow was to learn to identify emotions and to also determine what they made me think. I needed this help because I *did* have trouble identifying my emotions—particularly ones that I felt were unacceptable, like anger and sadness. I also had trouble identifying what I told myself when I felt those unacceptable emotions.

That fateful day, Zane took out a pen and paper and wrote it all down for me. I've now lost that paper, but I carried it around with me for months and months. It went something like this:

Start with an event that made you feel bad about yourself or your situation. For the first time I went through the Downward Arrow, I picked the time my husband shot me a mean look when I didn't do a very good job of docking the boat. It was a rather benign event but epitomized the type of interaction I tried to avoid with him.

How did I feel when he gave me the look? *Guilty for not being better at driving the boat.* (Downward arrow)

Why did I feel guilty? *Because I disappointed him.* (Downward arrow)

What did it say about me that I disappointed him? *That I wasn't very capable.* (Downward arrow)

How did I feel about not being very capable? *Humiliated.* (Downward arrow)

What did it say about me that I felt humiliated? *That I didn't deserve anything better.* (Downward arrow)

How did I feel about not deserving anything better? *Sad that I didn't deserve more.* (Downward arrow)

What did it say about me that I didn't deserve more? *That I was worthless.* (Downward arrow)

How did I feel about being worthless? *That there was no hope.* (Downward arrow)

What did it saw about me that there was no hope? *That I shouldn't be alive.*

I couldn't think of anything lower than that. So Zane said, "If you don't dock the boat the way he wants you to, you go all the way to 'I shouldn't be alive.' That's a very lonely place, isn't it? That puts a lot of pressure on you to behave in a way that keeps you from feeling like you shouldn't exist."

And he was right. I put a tremendous amount of expectation on myself to keep my husband happy and my life running smoothly so that I could minimize the times I felt like I was nothing. The problem was that I was terminally unhappy; I really wanted to leave my marriage and upend everything I'd worked so hard at keeping together. If there was ever a situation where I was going to be on the receiving end of mean looks and fighting, this was it. But there was no way I could go through with the divorce if it meant that I would feel worthless on the other side.

So I went through the Downward Arrow process again. This time, I used the divorce as my event.

How would he react to me asking for a divorce? *Angry.* (Downward arrow)

How did I feel about making him angry? *Afraid.* (Downward arrow)

What did it say about me that I was afraid? *That I did something wrong.* (Downward arrow)

How did I feel about doing something wrong? *Guilty.* (Downward arrow)

What did it say about me that I felt guilty? *That I was purposefully hurting my family for the sake of hurting them.* (Downward arrow)

How did I feel about purposefully hurting my family? *That I was a bad mother and a bad person.* (Downward arrow)

What did it say about me that I was a bad mother and a bad person? *That I deserved to have my children taken away and be unhappy forever.* (Downward arrow)

How did I feel about deserving to have my children taken away and being unhappy forever? *Hopeless. Worthless.* (Downward arrow)

What did it say about me that there was no hope and that I had no worth? *That there was no point to my existence. My life meant nothing. I meant nothing. I* was *nothing.* (Downward arrow)

It was an awful, terrifying place to be—feeling like I had no reason to live, my children would be better off without me, I had no hope, and I had no future.

Luckily, Zane also had a solution.

The beauty of the Downward Arrow, Zane explained, was that I could climb back up the staircase of downward arrows. If I started with the truth that I was already alive and should stay that way, *then I was somebody.*

And if I was somebody, *I wasn't worthless.*

And if I had worth, *then I deserved to be happy.*

And if I deserved to be happy, *then I wasn't a bad person.*

And if I wasn't a bad person, *then I wasn't purposefully and selfishly hurting my family for the sake of hurting them.*

And if I wasn't purposefully hurting my family, *then I didn't need to feel guilty.*

And if I didn't need to feel guilty, t*hen I wasn't doing anything wrong by asking for the divorce.*

Of course, I couldn't control whether or not my husband was going to be angry. He would feel however he felt, whether that was angry or sad or depressed. But I could control how I felt about my decisions and about my worth. I could learn that a negative reaction to me didn't mean I was nothing.

Fast forward another three years…my divorce was complete, I was (for the first time in 14 years) off anti-depressants, and I was feeling very good about my life's direction. I was also sitting by a campfire in northeastern Wisconsin with a group of motorcyclists, friends of friends, people I barely knew. I overheard the woman next to me talking about an "Arrows Up" club. I asked her to explain it.

Apparently the very unofficial Arrows Up club started by accident when, according to local boating legend, a boater had a terrible accident that resulted in his craft hanging upside down in some trees along a river bank. He was relatively unharmed and when his boat finally made it out of the trees and back to him, several of his friends taped big arrows on the side of it to remind him which side should always be pointing up.

Since that time, the group has awarded Up Arrows to various friends for outrageous or outstanding deeds – anything from drinking too much tequila (the Cuervo Gold Arrow) to finding their way to a campsite by boat, late at night (the Canal Sniffer Arrow). They've joked about putting Up Arrows on their coffins when the die so their pallbearers don't mess things up. I like their thinking.

That Wednesday, what seems like a lifetime ago, I needed to go through the exercise of the Downward Arrow—even now, I credit that experience in Zane's office with showing me that I could be okay if I got divorced. I wouldn't die and my children wouldn't wither on the vine. Without that support, I would have continued to stop short of seeking the very best life for myself and my children. I would have continued to feel like I didn't deserve better. I would have continued to feel utterly hopeless and paralyzed with fear. But that simple shift in logic, that very basic change in assumptions about my own life, showed me a way out of the pit in which I was wallowing.

And now the Up Arrow gives me ideas about celebrating accomplishments and successes. Maybe this year I get the Tomato Pie Arrow for my monstrous vegetable garden. Or perhaps I get the Pink Helmet Arrow for always wearing my pink motorcycle helmet (complete with black and silver swirls), regardless of how girlie it looks to hard-core bikers.

Any of us who have been stuck on the downward arrow path (whether it's been for years or just a few days) and who have fought to climb back up those steps deserve some kind of recognition. Because we know it's not easy to discard those negative thoughts and replace them with ones that we've been told are selfish or unrealistic.

What should we call it?

Touching the Trees

Chapter Nine
Battleship

I'll be honest—I had no idea how bad it would feel to get divorced. I wasn't even remotely prepared for the tremendous emotional upheaval or the gut-wracking contractions of an adult-sized rebirth.

I've done my best to avoid conflict forever, a disservice that became evident as soon as the last married goodbye left my lips. I was no more prepared to do battle with my ex-husband as I was to sing with the opera or debate world leaders on healthcare reform. For about nine months, every single interaction with him was a conflict—a cranium-meets-concrete-wall conflict that left me gulping for air and wondering if I could ever stand up straight again after being curled into a ball for so long.

A lot of our conflicts were about money. A lot. More than that, though, they were about control.

And I wanted some, for once.

When my boys were little I came across an electronic Battleship game at a garage sale. It was a self-contained, blue plastic carrying case of white ships and red pegs. When I got it home, put new batteries in it and turned it on, the world of strategic games opened wide for those kids. We spent hours playing—each boy placing his ships just so, setting up coordinates, and trying to sink each other's (or my) fleet first.

Once one of us was able to land a missile, it was just a matter of deciding whether to go right, left, up, or down to shoot another one. If the second missile hit as well, it was easy to shoot down the line until the whole ship was blown up. Once a ship was a goner (it actually said, "That ship's a goner!"), the game would make this horrible bellow to announce the fact that the destruction was complete.

Although I was somewhat decent at electronic battleship for a short time in the year 2000—it was a lot like Lite Brite but with ships and loud noises—I've never excelled at strategy games in general. I'm not sure why they're so hard for me except that I don't have that cut-throat instinct, even in make-believe. And the unfortunate by-product of not being good at strategy is that it's then very easy to let myself get cornered and blown up.

My father was a business major in college with a psychology minor. When I was a child, that psych minor of his meant that he was good at getting me and my siblings to do what he wanted us to. He took great pride in showing my mom "how it was done" by using words and argument to get us to behave. "Reverse psychology" and "manipulation" became as much our disciplinarians as his fraternity paddle and her flyswatter.

There was so little that was beneath him. I was a fairly talented violin player in middle and high school. When the time came (as it does for fairly good musicians) to upgrade my instrument to something better, he came into my room, sat on the edge of my bed, and explained in great detail how he was willing to buy me the new violin if—and only if—I agreed to practice every day and become a professional musician. Since I wanted nothing more than that new violin, I agreed to his condition—at age 11. Needless to say I failed, although I was pretty decent until college.

His pattern of adding conditions, often impossible conditions, to everything I asked of him became commonplace. I couldn't date an African American or a Jew or I wouldn't get any of the money my grandfather left me. I couldn't major in English education in college unless I switched to a less-expensive school (I didn't switch, but did change my major to the much less marketable English Composition). I couldn't sleep with my boyfriend (ahem, *again*—as my parents dramatically found out after reading my mail) before marriage or I would be disowned. I couldn't have a wedding unless I saved him money by graduating from college early. It went on and on until I felt like I had no choice but to escape him by marrying the boy who felt obligated to me.

So I got married and, eventually, got myself into the same corners as before. I couldn't go away for a girls' weekend without making all the arrangements for childcare and meals. I couldn't work outside the home without taking all the childcare responsibility on myself. I felt like I had to justify everything. Towards the end of our marriage, I couldn't go out with my friends without accounting for my whereabouts and conversations. And when even that wasn't good enough for him, I couldn't write emails or make telephone calls without him cyber-spying.

My husband made it difficult to leave him until he was ready for me to leave (read: until he'd moved on to someone else). And even then he gave me impossible choices to make. He wanted the house and 50% custody of our three kids. In a rare attempt at pushback, I told him no. He could have either the house or 50% custody but not both. He told me I was a bad mom for wrecking our family and I believed him because I still allowed the Downward Arrow to control my decisions at times. So he got both.

At one point I asked him to permanently switch weekends with me so that our son could play with his friend—the son of the man who'd been a great friend to me during that time and to whom I'd become attracted. He refused. When I asked for a portion of a bonus payment, he threatened to cut my alimony. When I asked him to co-sign a mortgage for me while we were separated, he threatened to cancel the closing unless I agreed to give him an interest in my house. When I gave him four months' notice of a working weekend trip—another reason to switch weekends with me—he told me that it wasn't his fault I was choosing my volunteer obligations over my children. It went on and on until the divorce was final.

I know I got stuck out of fear. With my dad, I was afraid of not getting that violin, so I gave in. I was afraid of starting over at a new college, so I gave in. I was afraid of getting disowned, so I...pretended to give in and snuck around more carefully.

With my husband, I was afraid that I really wasn't capable of taking care of the house on my own, so I gave in. I was afraid that he would leave me destitute and take the kids completely away, so I gave in. I gave and I gave and I gave...but in the end, did as much damage to myself as he and my dad did.

A lot of my ships were sunk over the years. There was a lot of horrible bellowing and a lot of Maydays. My latest mantra is, "What can anyone really do to me if I don't let them?" Sure, they can snipe and launch verbal missiles and try to make me feel bad about myself and my choices, but what can they really do to me? I have to believe that the answer is nothing, *if I don't let them.*

No, I'm not a great strategic mind and yes, I gave up more than I wanted to in the divorce. But the game is over and, for all intents and purposes, I've won.

I've won because I've learned to forgive myself for losing. I've won because I've learned how to avoid losing in the future. And I've won because, despite all the fighting, I'm happier than before.

Chapter Ten
Yeses and Nos

So…there's a little bit more that needs to be said about my father.

Through the years my mom has tried to explain him to me by saying things like, "He's an only child," "His mother wasn't very warm," "He wanted to be a musician but his dad wouldn't let him." All of that was supposed to make me feel better when he was unable to nurture, empathize, or listen with any compassion at all.

In the early years of my marriage I didn't see any comparison between my husband and my father. In fact,

I thought they were opposites. Or if not opposites, then I believed that my husband had the drive that I admired in my father but also the emotional capacity he lacked.

That worked well until my husband and I started at moving at different paces. I remember the day I asked my husband to slow down, quit working seven days a week, and just relax with me. We had moved to Cleveland and I wanted to take a few hours on a beautiful Saturday afternoon to walk to Lake Erie from our house. When he said no, I remember feeling like I couldn't keep up with him anymore. I lost my grip on the quest, went on the walk alone, and fell back into a support position.

It was from there—way back there—that I started seeing similarities between the two men. I started seeing that sometimes I was not only the woman who was too tired to stand up to her husband, but I was still the little girl that couldn't defy her dad.

Remember playground games?

Simon Says: Simon says move ahead two steps. Simon says move ahead one more. Now touch your head. Uh-oh, I didn't say "Simon Says." Go back to the beginning!

Blind Man's Bluff: Warmer, you're getting warmer…oops, colder…now you're warmer again, warmer…warmer…hot… you got me!

Marco Polo, Mr. Fox, Duck Duck Goose (or as they say in the Upper Midwest, Duck Duck Grey

Duck)—we learn these games as kids. They teach us to listen, follow directions, go back to Start when we mess up, and share the power. One kid gets to be Simon, Marco, or It until he or she loses the turn. Then someone else gets to be in charge. It's how the games work. It's how life is supposed to work. Take turns, listen carefully, make adjustments, learn from your mistakes, and try again.

But there's always someone who doesn't follow the rules. The kids call them poor sports, brats, bullies, or even "that weird kid that lives down the street." Those bossy ones make the game unenjoyable for everyone else just so that they can be in charge. They rarely care that the other kids would rather quit than put up with a tyrannical poop-head. They just do what they want because it makes them feel good.

Those kids also get older, get married, and have kids of their own. But sometimes they're still poop-heads.

A few years ago, instead of writing down all the things I couldn't stand about my husband, which I did later anyway, I decided to write down all the qualities I wanted in a partner. It was a Macy's wish list, an emotional gift registry. It was a way for me to move forward rather than focus on all that was going or had gone terribly wrong. I didn't want it to be a box that I would shove all prospective dates in to see if they fit, but it was a way for me to remind myself of what I needed.

Here's my list. I titled it "Expectations":

- Accepts me
- Follows through
- Participates in important life events
- Doesn't try to exert control over my feelings
- Believes that I know myself
- Doesn't want to hurt me if I go against his wishes
- Is emotionally trustworthy
- Is smart, funny
- Whose first reaction is "Sure"
- Gives me time and space to myself

I later went back and put two question marks beside *Whose first reaction is "Sure"*. I can't remember why I did it then, but maybe it's the same reason I would do it now.

It's because I crave Yes. Yes, if you think it's a good idea, that's good enough for me. Yes, if you want to drive all night to see your family, that's great. Yes, if you need to have this…yes, if you want to do this…just plain yes. Yes is approval and yes is trust. But even when I've needed a yes from someone else, I've been trained to accept no.

My father had a way of taking what I wanted or needed and twisting it to become what he thought was a better idea. I wasn't allowed to fail or fall down or make mistakes. I also wasn't allowed to succeed without him taking credit for guiding me to that conclusion.

I loathed having to ask his opinion on anything because, without question, it was different from mine and his was right. I never heard, "Yes, you should major in whatever you want." "Yes, I would love to meet your new boyfriend." "Yes, have a great time out tonight." "Yes, you're doing a great job raising your kids." None of that ever happened. Not once. The only thing he was genuinely proud of me for accomplishing was bearing children. I think it's because it's the one thing in this world that I could do better than him. I was borne of the playground bully.

Then I married one, although his bullying didn't start until later. Picking out every day china for our wedding registry, I can remember deferring to his opinion because, since it was different from mine, it must be right. I wanted these off-white plates with the slightest scallop around the edge. They were timeless and simple. They would match nearly anything we might pair them with then or in the future. He thought they were too girlie and absolutely refused to consider them. So we ended up with beige plates with country-blue rims that I had to decorate my kitchens around for the next ten years. His opinion was stronger than mine and I didn't want to start our life together fighting about plates. So he got to be Simon, out of turn.

From my father and from him I learned that no meant my idea, process, need, or want was most likely wrong. Even as a married woman and a mother, I often believed that I wasn't capable of making a decision on my own.

I hit a particularly low period when we lived down south. This was the move I didn't want to make because I had both 17- and 5 month-old babies, but I wasn't the breadwinner and the breadwinner had a job there, so we went. One day, I had a rare opportunity to leave the kids with a sitter and go to the mall alone. I even had a birthday gift card to the department store. I could be free for a little while, have a Coke, eat a pretzel with cheese, shop, and relax.

Only I couldn't. I got to that store and was unable to make a decision about what to get for myself. My husband was unavailable at work, I had no girlfriends to call (nor a cell phone, for that matter), and my heart was pounding. So I stood at a jewelry counter. Then I stood among clothes racks. Then I stood in the middle of the kitchen section. I was so afraid of wasting my gift card on something that wasn't right that I couldn't spend it.

So I didn't. I drove home, sent the sitter on her way, and told my husband we could just use money the next time we needed clothes for the kids.

To be fair, my husband might not have disapproved of what I bought. I suspect he really didn't care one way or another about what I spent that gift card on. But so many other decisions had been so one-sided that I couldn't take that chance. I was tired of being wrong and I didn't have enough reserves to fight for yes if I needed to.

His no took many forms. It was often a question, "Are you sure that's what you want to do?" It was like a teacher saying, "Maybe you should think about that until you get the right answer." Sometimes it was just a look. My husband was so good at shutting me up with a look that I went ahead and unoriginally named it "The Mean Look". I have a picture of the time he gave me that look while I was trying to dock the boat. It still kind of scares me. Or no was final approval. "You research going to South Dakota with the kids and we'll (I'll) decide later."

Recently no was described to me this way: Picture yourself walking in the woods with your spouse or special other. You veer off the trail to pick a beautiful wildflower. Within a few steps your partner yells, "Are you out of your flipping mind? Why is that flower so important that you have to walk away from me?" You think to yourself that, of course, a flower isn't more important than this special person; it was just pretty and there didn't seem to be any reason not to pick it. But you sense the no, you feel stupid and wrong, and you retreat back to being in-step and on-track.

You learn that every time you take the path less traveled by (thank you, Robert Frost) you get attacked with emotional or verbal poison darts. Simon didn't say you could do that. You're a screw-up. Go back to the beginning and try to get it right this time.

Now that I don't live with perpetual Simon and his nos, I embrace yes whenever I can. I give yes to my kids. Sometimes it means, "I want you to have fun with your friends." Yes also means, "Sure, try making dinner that way" (even if I am fairly certain it won't work). Yes means that I value their decision-making abilities and I trust them. In the long run, I believe they will learn more from a thoughtful, well-considered yes, whether their decision ultimately results in a success or a failure, than from a no.

I also give yes to my friends now. "I can make it to the party…the bar…the movie" (or any one of a number of events that I had to pass on before). I give out a lot of yeses now and get a lot in return.

I also save special yeses for myself. Yes, I can install a kitchen faucet. Yes, I can till up some yard and plant a vegetable garden. Yes, I can raise happy kids. Yes, I'm capable of making decisions for myself.

Yes, I am. Yes, you are, too.

Chapter Eleven
Mine

One of the side-effects of being in a support role during my husband's epic quest for upper management was that while I was keeping the campfire going, he was roaming, exploring, and plundering villages. Okay, not really. But he was bringing home the spoils of his work. Like a caveman dragging back a wild pig or a world trader tossing a sack of gold over the threshold, my husband did a good job of providing for our family.

I did a good job of keeping the family running while he was gone.

Touching the Trees

The problem was that he felt like I didn't give him enough credit for being the one who provided for us financially and I felt like he didn't give me enough credit for providing everything else. One constant in our house was that we both felt like we did more than the other.

There's a scene in the kids' movie *Finding Nemo* when dozens of seagulls are on a dock waiting for a morsel of food, fish or otherwise. When they see potential dinner, they all squawk "Mine! Mine! Mine!"

No matter how many times I watch that scene, I'm still a little afraid for the two fish that are trying to survive the pecking. But I also feel bad for the seagulls that won't get a fish. Maybe they aren't the most aggressive. Maybe they aren't the smartest. Maybe they just got busy doing something else and missed their chance. But the end result is the same: They have nothing they can claim as their own.

I have felt like the seagull that missed dinner.

For the last decade of our marriage, my husband referred to various possessions as "his". This was ironic, since we got married so young and there wasn't one thing we owned that was his prior to the wedding. Everything we had was "ours" from the get-go. For the first seven years, we both worked, we both contributed, we both decided what to buy, and we both were enthralled with the idea that we shared everything. But then we started a family, I quit working, and that all changed.

I take some responsibility for his sense of entitlement. I grew up in a family run by an unpredictable, controlling father. You didn't dare lay claim to anything, including your own desires and dreams, because if he didn't think they were what you should have, you didn't get to have them. Period. So I was a little prewired to acquiesce. If my husband wanted to squawk "Mine!" it was generally okay with me from the very beginning of our relationship (hence the country blue plates).

Then I got busy. My second son was born a year and six days after my first son. Before my second son turned one, we moved from one state to another and back. I didn't have time to retain any memories, let alone maintain my status as an equal partner in the marriage. He was busy leveraging each long week into a promotion, each promotion into a raise, and each raise into a means to have more stuff. And that stuff, little by little, became "his". He made all the money, occasionally spent it just how he wanted to, and I was too exhausted push back and remind him that it was supposed to be ours. I couldn't keep up with his ability to claim fish, so I gave up caring whether I got any or not.

As the years went on, he pronounced his ownership of things randomly and somewhat unconsciously. The kids would scribble on the wall and it was, "Who wrote on my wall?" They would vomit in the family room and he'd be angry that they'd messed up his couch. One night my daughter spilled milk on the kitchen table during dinner and he yelled at her to quit messing up his things (I chose not to point out that it was actually *him* crying over the spilled milk). It was subtle but insinuating. Mi casa was not su casa. Our house, and everything in it, was his.

When I initiated the divorce from him, it was less a negotiation and more a process of him deciding what he'd give me. I was initially excited to finally have my independence from him—my own space, my own decision-making powers, and my own life filled with my own things. I got all that, except that I also retained custody of the nagging sense that none of it was really mine because I wasn't working and he was "giving" me spousal maintenance. Technically, it was all paid for by him. Technically, I hadn't contributed more than a speck of income in 15 years. So was that what defined ownership?

When I moved into my new house, I bought a small table with matching stools. This was my first completely independent furniture purchase…ever. It's the set that, even now, I love to run my fingers over to feel the smoothness of the wood. But what felt really good to me was that the *process* of buying the new table and stools was mine. I picked them out, charged them to my credit card, and made arrangements for a friend to help me get them home.

We set it all up, positioning the table just how I wanted it, and I placed a scented candle in the center. This table looked like "me" and it completed the room just how I want it to. Then the bill came and I paid it off with my alimony.

Which made me wonder if the table could ever feel like mine, even if the process did.

I've heard a very compelling argument from Zane that the answer to that question—and the question of whether or not my new house, my car, and even that table with the scented candle centerpiece are mine—is a "Heck yes!" I gave up jobs and potential jobs for the sake of my husband's career and our family. I was a committed stay-home parent by mutual agreement (and a little bit of default) and I was an often-effective fort holder-downer so that he could travel, work late, go to grad school, entertain clients, and sleep in on the weekends. For every long hour or week that he worked, I worked those same hours or more taking care of our family. Given the sheer magnitude of amount of work I did, a reasonable person could say that I earned every penny I continue to get.

Even given that, though, it is not easy to discard years and years of believing that the money I have isn't mine. It may take me more time to believe that the alimony that shows up in my checking account every two weeks is something I deserve and have earned. That transition is one that will be complete only with the passage of time and some income of my own. It'll happen eventually, though. It's already started.

Because here's what I realized as I was contemplating the question of how to determine if something is mine: Maybe for a lot of things it doesn't matter. Regardless of whose paycheck bought my groceries last week, whose name is on my car loan, or whose 401K distribution funded my house down payment, they are merely possessions that inhabit a world I'm creating for myself.

Seagulls don't worry about where the fish came from. If they squawk "Mine!" and get the fish, the fish is theirs.

Chapter Twelve
Mirrors

I'm not a big proponent of infidelity, not just for the obvious reason that it eventually hurts a bunch of people, but because it means that some disconnect should have been taken care of much earlier. Cheating is a symptom of a relationship that's in serious trouble or, frankly, already over.

In a sane world, someone who's contemplating having an affair with a person other than his or her spouse or committed partner should take a moment before slipping between the sheets and ask, "Why am I doing this?"

That almost never happens, of course, because there's a reason a person craves and then seeks out companionship or sex outside a supposedly committed relationship. It's because something vital to the life of that relationship is missing.

I get all that. I didn't when I first found out I'd been cheated on, though. I remember sitting in our first couples therapist office wondering why my husband's cheating was somehow my fault. I wondered how I could have been any better of a wife than to give up my dream job, move away from our families, and give him whatever he needed or wanted. I'd even scaled back my own desires for affection and attention because he didn't have those same feelings.

What could I have done differently? In reality, probably nothing. I didn't have any way to understand there was a problem and even less ability to communicate openly about it. He, too, wasn't able to express why he did it. Although we both should have been able to discern that he wanted out of the marriage—his infidelity was a big clue—we didn't.

So we plugged away at it for many more years and had three great children.

Then at some point between diaper changes, preschool carpools, and t-ball, I started having those same desires to stray. There were times when I was so lonely, so desperate, and so hollow that a glance from the guy in the car next to me would be enough to mitigate my sadness for a little while.

There's a part of me that wonders if that's what my husband felt when he cheated. Was he that lonely and unhappy? Or was he just wired like so many other Alpha males—seeking the conquest and sowing the seed? I don't know and, now, it doesn't matter.

I just know that when I started enjoying my time away from home much more than my time with him, and when I felt a compulsion to flirt, even with subtlety, with any guy anywhere that would make eye contact, there was a big problem.

Because I needed to take a long look at myself and decide whether the attention I could get was worth feeling like I was just like him.

Try this: Using your "off" hand (I'm right-handed, so I use my left), hold a pen and begin writing backwards, in cursive. It may take a couple of tries, but eventually you'll see that if you write in a way that feels natural, your handwriting, when held up to a mirror, looks freakishly like your regular handwriting.

I figured this trick out during one uncomprehendingly boring event when I was in college…or high school. It was so boring I don't even remember. I spent an inordinate amount of time that day practicing writing the alphabet and my name and it was kind of interesting to realize that I had a left-handed backwards person inside of me. That insight nearly kept me awake.

Now put down the paper and look in the mirror. That face looking back at you is the same one that's

Touching the Trees

been looking back at you forever. But that's not what you really look like. The woman in my mirror parts her hair on the left and her sunglasses always slant to the right because her ears are unbalanced. She winks better with her left eye, which is also slightly greener. She's left-handed, like I always wanted to be. She tends to stick out her right hip when she's trying to make a point.

But she's me, right?

One time I stared into my own eyes for a little too long. It started because I was curious as to the exact color of my eyes and, apparently, had nothing better to do during a rare mommy bathroom break. So I sat on a bathroom counter, trying to keep from bruising my knee on the faucet, and just stared. Turns out, although my driver's license says my eyes are green, I realized after a few minutes that they're a conglomeration of blues and browns that shimmy themselves into looking that way.

But what also happened after a while of sitting in that position, staring into my own eyes, is that I saw something a little frightening. So I blinked and looked away.

No, I didn't see any terrible monster or horrific urges. Instead, I saw complacency. I saw settling for less. For the first time, I saw my own uncensored unhappiness and I was embarrassed. I couldn't make eye contact because I was lying to myself that the life I had was enough. Good thing I was never a criminal or a poker player. My "tell" was pronounced and profound.

It's hard not being comfortable in your own skin. Until just recently, I felt like that almost all the time. I didn't fit the mold—ever. I was the tomboy who started the girls' golf team at my high school but who also wore formal dresses and played violin in front of audiences at the local university. I was in the college honors program but also (for a short time) a pregnant pom-pom girl. I wanted independence, but felt like I could only get it by getting married.

Even as an adult, I felt like I didn't fit the mold. I was a middle school English teacher (in a very old-school school that particular year) who wanted all my students to learn to love language rather than just memorize for the standardized tests. Because of that, each day I had a different playful task for them. My favorite was when they had to spell aloud everything they wanted to say in class. "T-e-a-c-h-e-r, c-a-n I p-a-s-s o-u-t s-p-e-l-l-i-n-g t-e-s-t-s?" Those poor kids had to think to spell and think to listen. I thought it was great; the administration didn't agree.

I was a wife who wanted to be a strong partner, but stayed married to and had children with the man who cheated on me several times before our fifth anniversary. I was the parent who felt like a failure because my mom's group was highly focused on cleanliness, safety, and shoes while I was more concerned with my kids learning how to feed themselves, how to avoid an owie the second time around, and how to grip their toes in the grass and carpet in order to steady their wobbly toddler legs.

Looking back, it's no wonder I couldn't maintain eye contact in the mirror. I was a fraud nearly every day of my life. But I wasn't a fraud because I was different from other people. I was a fraud because I didn't embrace and celebrate my differences.

I didn't always stand up for what was right for me and my children. More often than not, I believed I was wrong simply because someone else thought they were right. I knew that the woman in my mirror didn't resemble the one that other people saw. I just didn't know what to do about it.

Then I went to a bar and met a guy.

That sounds a little cliché, doesn't it? *My whole world changed when I met a guy at a bar.* And it really did, but not for the usual reasons.

See, a few years ago I lost about 30 pounds. I needed to. My daughter was five and I was way past being able to pass off the extra weight as baby fat. My health wasn't great—lots of stomach issues, sleep problems, neck pains, etc. I'd blown through my 40th birthday unhappy with myself and was increasingly depressed despite those good medications. Basically, something needed to change and my weight was it.

So I joined a weight-loss program and slowly started losing weight. I mean s-l-o-w-l-y...I'm not one of those people who enjoys a big initial drop then steadies into a two-pound loss per week. I started with two pounds per week and never deviated. By my 41st birthday, I was down four sizes and felt great. More than great, I felt hot and desirable and smart and funny. I started to like the woman in my mirror just a little, if for no other reason than she could wear expensive jeans…and a *belt*.

But all was not rosy. My husband still didn't have much time for me or the kids. I begged him to cut back on coaching (an additional 14-hour per week commitment) and he decided to coach anyway. Twice I also begged him to have sex with me and he refused. One of those two times he finally relented after I started crying, and I pretended to be grateful, but was disgusted with myself for going through with it. So, even having a new body didn't turn me completely into the person I wanted to be. I just looked a little more like her.

Then came a fateful November. My husband was in California for a work/golf/drinking trip with clients for the week. He was due home on a Friday night so I made plans to go out with a girlfriend to a bar to relax from a week of non-stop kid duty. At about 5 pm that night, as I sat at my son's hockey practice all dolled up to go out, he called from San Diego and said he wasn't going to be home that night because they'd missed their flight. They'd been too drunk to get to the airport on time. He was really sorry and all, but there wasn't anything he could do. He'd probably be home on Saturday if he could get a flight.

I told him it was fine, hung up and immediately called a babysitter.

A couple hours and beers later, while my friend (who was single) hung out with a tall blonde guy, I hung out at the bar playing wingman with his wingman. This extra guy and I stood there for a while, sipping our beers, watching the television over the bar, eavesdropping on our friends, but not saying much of anything. Then I started talking (I have no idea about what), he started laughing, and we hit it off like crazy.

All of a sudden I felt beautiful, witty, and charming. In the span of a couple of hours, I morphed into the woman I thought I'd seen lurking behind my eyes in the bathroom mirror. She was authentic, not scared. She wasn't afraid to look good and feel good, despite the long week and longer early evening. And I really liked wearing her around like she was me.

My bar buddy and I exchanged phone numbers and email addresses at the end of the night. I went home to my empty bed and stayed awake nearly all night wondering what had just happened. How had I gone from a frustrated stay-home-parent to a woman who had exchanged personal information with a complete stranger—and who felt good about it? How was it that, all of a sudden, I could look myself in the eyes and finally not be ashamed of what I saw there? Who was this woman?

I believe in fate and I believe that you can find a lesson in nearly everything that happens. And that night, regardless of how silly and trite it sounds, was a turning point for me.

I didn't have an affair with that guy. I didn't run away with him and let him solve all my problems. I did secretly email back and forth with him for about five weeks before I realized that he was just like my husband—self-absorbed, controlling, and awful to his wife—but in a different package. And I didn't want another person like that in my life. Everything in me rebelled against making that same mistake again. So, instead of becoming a statistic and using an affair to get out of a marriage, I got the courage to head back to counseling, wrote a letter telling my husband that I was done being married to him (this was the last clue I needed to be sure of that decision), and prepared to become the person I'd always wanted to be.

Of course, the rest of the process wasn't simple or easy. My husband didn't believe that I could leave him without giving him another chance or twenty. He didn't believe I didn't have an "emotional" affair with every guy to cross my path from that point forward. He didn't believe that I knew myself. He underestimated the woman in the mirror.

Now that it's all over—the ink is dry and the marriage with its suffocating sadness has dwindled to a much less painful memory—I'm not afraid to look into my own eyes anymore. Sometimes I stare long and hard at that woman who wanted to come join me. Then I reach for the mirror, and take her hands.

Touching the Trees

Chapter Thirteen
Plastic Bags

There's a problem with trying to leave a person who likes power. I thought it would be good enough for me to tell my husband that it was time for us to be done being married. I really thought that would work. Sure, we'd have some painful moments when we split up twenty years of stuff, but we were both reasonable adults and, surely, he didn't want me around if I didn't want to be there.

I underestimated the level of control he needed. I overestimated my ability to avoid the Downward Arrow. Both of those things nearly broke my will to search anymore for myself and the emotional freedom that had eluded me for so long. I began suffocating.

    We must have all had a hard time living through being a kid. The number of safety products developed after I'd already gone through my growth spurts is astounding—car seats, lead-free paint, walkers without wheels, big wheels with parent handles, kid leashes, emission controls, closely-spaced slats, Jarts made out of bean bags instead of spikes, Mr. Yuck, fabric-covered recliner footrests, anti-scald faucets, warning labels about everything...
    But one potentially lethal hazard that science and industry have never seemed to be able to do away with is the plastic bag.
    It's quite possible that my second favorite childhood death-defying activity was wearing plastic bags on my head. (My first was standing behind cars and inhaling exhaust fumes.) I'd put those plastic bags on and twist them into intricate chignons or let them hang down my back like so much Cher hair. Wearing plastic bags for fake movie-star coifs was like wearing Bugles corn chips for fingernails. At my house, it was also like wearing chunks of 2x4s, held onto my feet with yarn, as high heels.
    I'm sure at various points in time my mom reminded me and my siblings not to put plastic bags over our heads. I'm sure she re-stated the Surgeon General's

warning in a worn-out mom monotone. "Don't put that bag over your head. You'll suffocate." That was her job, just as it was our job to make playthings out of anything handy and slightly dangerous or edible.

I outgrew plastic bag hair and 2x4 sandals about the same time I got my period. (But I'll admit to not outgrowing Bugles fingernails, because, to be honest…who has?)

As a parent, I've seen my own kids put plastic bags on their heads and I've repeated the same safety mantra my own mother did decades ago. Don't do it. You'll suffocate. You'll die.

Plastic bags do pose a real threat since about 25 children in the U.S. under the age of one die each year as a result of plastic bag asphyxiation. To be fair to plastic bag manufacturers, though, nearly all plastic bags carry a warning about the risks of suffocation. Also, if there's one thing moms leave the hospital knowing to say to their babies, it's "Get that bag off your head *right now!*"

In the last couple of years I've spent some time thinking about suffocation. Not the actual physical kind, because that would be creepy, but the emotional kind. In fact, the one word that could sum up the last 18 months of being married to my husband would be just that: suffocation. But I doubt he's the only spurned spouse inclined towards that. As you know, I'm no psychologist or behavioral scientist, but I'll wager a bag of pointy corn chips there's a pattern to be found in the actions of the spouse who doesn't want to be left. And the pattern resembles, very closely, suffocation by plastic bag.

Step one: You tell your spouse you would like to be finished being married to them. The spouse you want to leave, regardless of how many times you went to marriage counseling (in my case it was four—and I'm not talking four sessions. I mean four different therapists, four different years, two different cities, and two different decades), will look at you like you're a puppy butcher. There's no two ways around it. Sure, you'd been talking about divorce for 15 years. Sure, he knew you were unhappy and unfulfilled. Sure, there was no trust left. But he never thought you'd actually *do* it.

So your spouse will take arms of guilt and memories and hold them out like a big red Target bag at Christmas time. "See all this?" he'll ask. "This is our life. We've got fabulous kids who deserve a two-parent home. We've got nice things. We've got security. We've got our own family language and three-inch thick photo albums from each of the last twenty years. We belong together." Your spouse will ask you to peek into that bag—that history—just for a minute while he plans his next step.

And you will. Of course you will. You'll look back on your life together and think, "That time on the airplane when one of our kids was puking and you were a jerk to the flight attendant wasn't so bad." "We got through X, Y, and Z and had some good times afterward, so it must not have been that horrible, right?"

The plastic bag is working on you and it's not even over your head yet.

Step two: You decide to stick around for a while to sort things out. There was a lot of good that happened during your marriage. You laughed, you made love, and you fell asleep in each other's arms. You held one another close when his grandmother died. You cried together when you put the cat to sleep. As a unit, you experienced the birth of your children, their first days of school, and that magical afternoon when they didn't need training wheels anymore. You sweated your butts off on moving day and then flopped together on the carpet with cold beers and pizza that night. That was all good stuff. Those memories are the glue that held you together so long. They shouldn't be minimized.

But that itching you feel around the base of your neck? That's the bag closing in on you. You've moved beyond looking in it like it just fell down the chimney in winter—you're wearing that bag like a superhero cape or a great mound of Ginger Grant's red hair. You're flying high on all the good memories. You're also feeling sad. You're questioning yourself. Really, what's the ratio of unhappiness to happiness that justifies a divorce? At what point does the good outweigh the bad? And when, if ever, is it okay to tie the bag shut and leave it out for recycling?

Step three: Your spouse gets suspicious. He or she has had a little time to think now. Maybe it's been a few days or maybe it's been a couple of months since you said you're done. But they've come to the conclusion that there can't possibly be anything wrong with *them* to cause you to want a divorce. You must be under the influence of a lover, family members that have always hated them, friends that want you to party more, television, angry music, mental illness, emotional breakdown, alcohol, or boredom. There's just no logical reason why you won't stay married to someone as wonderful as him or her—someone who has given you so much and asked for so little. And you almost believe your spouse because, frankly, what person in their right mind would want to give up so much of the known—even with its frustrations and unhappiness—to delve into the unknown, an unknown that might just be worse? Most of us aren't gamblers on that grand of a scale.

And so your spouse (oh, so carefully) pulls the bag up and over your head while you're sleeping.

You don't feel it at first, maybe. It starts with a text here or there: "Hey, thinking of u! ☺" Or a phone call: "Hi, um, I was just wondering if you'd like to go on a date night this weekend. I already called a sitter." You'll notice far more encounters. Some of those special new times together will feel great because you've been begging your spouse for them for years. All that grocery shopping you did on your own? Now he wants to come and push the cart. Gifts, concert tickets, backrubs, day trips…all ways to convince you to stay. And all ways to crush your will to leave.

The plastic bag will slowly (or more quickly if you fight it), start cutting you off from the outside world and from yourself. In one of my friend's cases, the suffocation took the form of isolating him from his closest friends and family. The more he wanted to pull away, the more his wife bad-mouthed everyone he cared about. In my case, it took the form of cyber-spying. At Christmas one year, my husband found out (by looking at the history on my laptop) that I had an email address he wasn't aware of. Instead of taking that for what it was—that very clear sign that our marriage really was troubled—he took it to mean that I was incapable of managing my urge to leave him. So he bought software that turned over to him, like a drug-addled street snitch, all of the passwords to all of my accounts and documents.

I didn't realize this violation at first. I continued emailing that guy I'd met at the bar for a couple more weeks. I also emailed my friends about my guilt and frustrations. I kept writing poetry. I kept journaling—all for nine more months. It wasn't until he "just happened" to find out, within hours, that I'd emailed someone he'd forbidden me to email that I realized that something was amiss. I'm ashamed to say that it took me longer than it should have to call out his explanation of "somehow your email account just showed up on my smartphone." But eventually I did and realized that everything I'd written for months and months was up for grabs. I had no idea what he'd looked at, changed, or saved as ammunition. To this day he swears he didn't read anything except, occasionally, my emails. But I don't believe him.

The final tug on the knot around my neck—the one that caused me to see stars, gasp for a breath, and reach for a place to put my bluing head between my knees—was when he questioned me about my cell phone bill. He had brainwashed me so well into believing that it was okay for him to both monitor it and question me about it ("If you didn't have anything to hide, I wouldn't have to keep checking on you"), he didn't even bother lying about how long he'd been monitoring my incoming and outgoing calls. "Oh, since about Christmas." It was June. My suffocation was nearly complete.

Step four: Change your mind or change your address. You will eventually reach a critical turning point in the process of where you'll have to choose to stay or continue with your plan to leave. Neither option will sound viable because you won't be able to think rationally and your intuition will be starving for the freedom to feel its way through such an important decision.

Regardless of what you choose, though, the first thing you'll have to do is take that plastic bag off your head and breathe.

If you choose to stay, fold up the bag eight times or until it's as small as you can get it. Then shove it deep into the garbage can full of shrimp tails, buttered toast crust, and used tissues. Put the whole thing out at the curb, then go back inside the house and get some professional help. Confront your suffocator and figure out a way to regain your trust in him or his trust in you. It won't be easy and it won't be quick—after all, you've been through some pretty serious life-deprivation during this period. But, as another friend will attest, you *can* come back from wanting to leave your spouse, you *can* take the plastic bag off your head, and you *can* choose to trust. You can even be happy.

If you decide to leave, like I did, instead of folding the bag up neatly, rip it off with your fingernails and shred it in the lawn mower. You're going to need all the freedom and fresh air you can get as you pack up your memories, take care of the kids, and sort through the closets and junk drawers of your marriage for the things you want to keep and the things you never want to lay eyes on again.

On your way out of the marriage, though, remember this: A plastic bag can only suffocate you if you let it. So keep control of the Heftys, grab your Bugles and lace on some 2x4s. You've got work to do.

That work may take the form of finding professional help or putting together a solid support system of friends and family. It may mean thickening your skin and forcing yourself to remember that you aren't a bad person for wanting to be happy.

It may also mean finding a way out of your situation using your contacts, your interests, your hobbies, or whatever means necessary.

Chapter Fourteen
The Doorway Out

Speaking of finding a way out of a situation…

Several years ago, as part of fire prevention week at my kids' elementary school, we all went to an open house at the local fire station. All the bays were open and kids could climb up into the cabs of the fire engines, talk to the fire fighters, try on equipment, feel the weight of the fire hoses, and wear yellow plastic fire hats. But the highlight of the evening was the smoke house.

The smoke house was a simulator that children and adults could enter and feel what it was like to be trapped in a smoke-filled room. My boys were dying to try it out so we waited in line with other yellow-hatted kids and parents after we'd done everything else. I was hoping they'd change their minds. They didn't.

The way it worked was this: Once 10-12 people were in the trailer, fire fighters would fill the room with non-toxic smoke to simulate low visibility and stimulate a low level of panic. I'm not particularly claustrophobic, but even I felt my chest tighten up and my anxiety shoot through the roof when I could no longer see the door or the exit sign indicating that there *was* a door.

I'm sure the whole experience only lasted a few seconds, but it was enough to make me long for a way out. And that was the theme of my life for many years—longing for a way out.

It was very easy for me to develop tunnel vision as a stay-home parent when my kids were newborns, toddlers, and preschoolers. Every day was a whirlwind of mundane, rote activities to keep the kids alive, healthy, happy, and developmentally on-target. From the first awakening to the last kiss goodnight, I was focused on feeding, cleaning, wiping, changing, entertaining, and challenging my kids. As any parent knows, there are days when a shower is a luxury, as is a 15-minute bathroom break or a phone call.

Little by little, though, I found outlets that brought me into contact with other adults. I participated in play groups, took early childhood Mommy-and-me classes, and volunteered at preschool. After a while I became more active at my church and served on committees there.

Eventually, I stretched a little further, bought into a home-based business and found a great groove hosting parties and selling kitchen gadgets. I was more successful than I thought I would be, despite my tight schedule and babysitting fees.

Then I got pregnant with my third child, became nauseous at every party I worked, and had to quit.

A few years after that, I bought into a second home-based business, but the logistics of hosting events around three kids and my husband's work schedule was too much for me to handle. So I quit that one too.

Ironically, it was my husband that eventually showed me the way out of the haze.

Many years ago, my husband (a well-respected youth coach) was asked to join a newly-forming board of directors to lead a state-wide league. I remember well the night he came back from an initial meeting with the organization—I was irritated that he was home late and that I hadn't had a break all day from the kids. So it was with more than a little trepidation that I asked how the meeting went; I was sure he had gone ahead and taken the position, which would mean more time away from me and the kids.

But he surprised me. He said he knew he didn't have time to be on the board…and so he'd volunteered me to be on it instead.

I was flooded with contradictory emotions. My first thought was "Yes!" because I wanted something to do outside the home. My second thought was, "How dare you?" because I thought it was presumptuous of him to think of me as an extension of himself and offer me up to take his place. But my third thought was, "Why not?!" because having to go to meetings several times a year, in the evenings, was a dream come true. I could get out and, because of the nature of the organization, I would meet people from all over the city.

I couldn't wait to step up to close the garage door behind me and start this new venture. I finally had a way out of the daily grind. I finally had a chance to talk to other adults about something other than child-rearing. I wasn't tied to sales objectives or my husband's schedule—after all, he was the one who volunteered me. I was excited.

And all of that would have worked out great for us—I would have been satisfied with my few meetings a year and a minor role in the organization—had one seemingly insignificant event not taken place.

One night during a board meeting, one of the men proposed something that I didn't agree with. In previous meetings, I hadn't spoken nearly at all, so I listened as the other guys debated the pros and cons of his proposal. Finally, I couldn't take it anymore, cleared my throat, and suggested that—perhaps—it wasn't such a good idea after all. My heart was thumping; I was nearly hyperventilating. Although I'd been comfortable speaking in front of groups when selling, I felt awkward and uninformed speaking up about something I wasn't as sure about.

Then a surprising thing happened. All the guys stared for a moment, and then they agreed with me. It was a turning point—my voice was heard, my idea held weight, and I was *right*.

I was right.

I could breathe again.

My role on the board eventually expanded until I was making decisions that my husband, as a coach, had to abide by. I was asked to run for a leadership position, which I won. Then I was asked to be part of a national leadership group, which I did. My head swelled each time I earned another opportunity to show my strengths.

Then I would return home and revert back to being submissive and weak.

Little by little, I couldn't stand being right at my board meetings and wrong at home. I couldn't reconcile being one way—logical, thoughtful, and respected—as a board member and another way—meek, wary, and afraid—as a wife.

That position, the one for which my husband volunteered me, became my doorway out of my negative self-image and my destructive relationship.

Since the time I began working with that group, I've gained confidence by the bucketsful. That confidence gave me initial insight into the disconnect between how I was and how I wanted to be.

Success in a new arena can give us the strength to make the decisions that propel us forward. While we may still need to remind ourselves of this when situations turn tough, by finding a doorway out we can learn that it's possible to succeed on our own merit.

You may be looking for something—a new path, a better relationship, or a clearer sense of self. Any or all of that is possible if you're willing to say goodbye to your fears, welcome challenges, and step through the doorway of change.

Chapter Fifteen
Traveling by Anger

    For my twentieth wedding anniversary—the one that began with a mediation meeting and ended with touching his trees—I got my husband a card. It was blank inside, which put plenty of pressure on me to decide how best to craft the last words of our marriage.

    Among other things, I told him that we should both think of this parting as a beginning of something better. I wrote that I was grateful for the anger (clarification—I was glad for my anger *at him*, not so much his anger *at me*) because it did what I'd been unable to do before: propel myself out the door and toward something different and hopefully better.

The pastor at my church said something interesting about anger. He relayed a story about an angry clergyman (I guess they're human after all) and how this man was told to "make friends" with his anger.

Although my pastor didn't give any concrete examples about how to do that, exactly, I knew what he was talking about. Anger is a friend when it picks you up at the bus stop and takes you home, fast. It's not such a good buddy when it sits there, gunning the engine and blasting the radio instead of getting into gear.

Despite all the rage and vitriol I feel still sometimes, and despite the fact that it only takes about three words from my ex-husband to send me spiraling down the arrows again if I'm not careful, I've learned that I can't live in anger for very long.

In the book *The 12 Secrets of Highly Creative Women: A Portable Mentor,* by Gail McMeekin, Barbara Waugh is quoted as saying, "I think a roadblock is a signpost instead of a barrier. Maybe it's telling you something…You will have a better life, feel happier and more empowered to do what you want to do, if you frame it that a roadblock is really an indicator. Frame it so that the person who is against you is actually holding a truth that is valuable for your path, and you'll have more wins."

For a lot of my life, I saw roadblocks as just that—roadblocks. When I faced conflict with my husband, whether it was a disagreement about (quite literally) what road to take or whether it was his outright anger at me for going against his wishes, I viewed that conflict as a sign that I should tiptoe quietly away from the battlefield and come up with a better plan for avoiding that situation again.

I saw other people's anger and my failure to overcome it as signs that I was wrong—in my perceptions, my feelings, and even my thoughts about the situation. And although many rational people would have seen roadblocks as indicators that I was in unhealthy situations, I saw them as signs that I was flawed, stupid, and incapable. Instead of fighting back, I retreated into compliance time after time, year after year.

I learned this coping skill, which grew out of a combination of passivity and fear, from watching my own parents interact. My dad had the kind of unpredictable fuse length that led the rest of the family to be always watchful and careful. There were days when we kids could feel free to be outgoing, funny, and creative. Then there would be days where we'd behave in the exact same way and trigger something in him that would send him into a controlling fit. It was virtually impossible to determine with any reliability what would set him off.

That unpredictability continued into our adulthood. Just a few years ago I was at my parents' house making popcorn for my kids. When my dad realized what I was doing, he marched into the kitchen, turned off the microwave, and tried to force me to read the directions on the box. He was livid that I thought I could operate the appliance simply by pushing the "popcorn" button on the control panel.

So if conflict is a signpost or an indicator that something needs to change, then what role does anger play in resolving that conflict? In my most personal relationships, unfortunately, conflict was usually accompanied by anger directed at me, so its role was that of roadblock. I don't think that always has to be the case, though.

Like most everyone, I felt anger growing up – ranging from getting mad at the other neighborhood kids if they were playing unfairly to a deeply-rooted sense of unfairness and fury at the expectations and constraints my parents put on me. I was never encouraged or allowed to express that anger, though, and someone else usually became even more angry at *me* if I did.

Once I found the man that I thought was able to take care of me emotionally, I married him and began suppressing any anger I felt toward him too. I suppressed it in the face of his rudeness, his disrespect, his physical straying, and his domination until I rarely felt it anymore. What little anger I dared to show inflamed his so much that I trained myself to remain passive. It was safer that way, just like it was growing up. My unhappiness grew and grew, though.

So he and I went to a marriage counselor's office—again. It was Zane's.

Despite being in couple's therapy those three times before, we never resolved the issues we had, which included the fundamental conflict between his quest for more money and status, my desire to be noticed and supported, as well as our complete dearth of trust.

As we sat there on Zane's couch (quite a while before I thought of him as the greatest therapist in the world, I'll admit), I whined about feeling underappreciated and he countered with his usual defense about needing to provide for our family. Finally Zane stopped us and said to me, "You've always had a choice to change this situation. You've chosen to allow this life to occur. You've made the decision to live like this, so you really can't blame him." I was devastated.

As my husband jumped to applaud Zane's "wisdom", all I could think was, "But I *didn't* choose this. Who would choose so much unhappiness?"

With a very heavy heart, I decided right then that I would never be able to leave—and that I'd need to be medicated for the rest of my life, with any antidepressant that would work, in order to stay. It was one of my saddest moments. I didn't believe Zane heard me and I knew my husband hadn't. I was alone.

We left that office and didn't go back as a couple ever again. But a year later, after more expectations and rejections from him, I reflected back on that feeling of needing to stay drugged up on anti-depressants just to tolerate a bad marriage and I finally—finally—started to feel something that resembled anger. I got a little mad at Zane for saying I was wrong. I got a little more mad at myself for being such a wimp. And I got mad at my husband for not noticing, or maybe not caring, what he was doing to me.

Then I used my anger, even in that infant form, as a vehicle for change.

There's something to be said for using anger appropriately. I didn't learn how to as a kid and I didn't learn how to in my marriage, but once I allowed myself to feel it again I realized that it was easy to sit in my anger for long stretches of time. I could roil and pace and fume just like anyone else, even to the point of exhaustion. That didn't feel right either, though.

Then I thought: Anger is a vehicle—a car, train, bus, or bicycle. It can get me from one place to another quickly if I let it (or more slowly if I let it simmer too long), but then I need to step out of it and make the best of the new place at which I've arrived.

I thought about that when I wrote the final card to my husband on our last anniversary. Like an overloaded Griswold station wagon, my anger had gotten me and my emotional baggage from one side of a transition to another. It had given me the push to change for the better but would be unwise to drag around with me everywhere I went.

Granted, I probably should have channeled my pent-up anger a little longer. I should have put in another tank of gas and driven that thing more effectively through the mediation and divorce process, but I couldn't at the time. I didn't want to live in anger for any longer than I needed to.

I've tried to maintain that degree of separation from my anger without giving it up altogether. It's not easy, though, because there are still so many constants to be angry about. But I've worked at letting go when necessary—getting out of the driver's seat of the anger car and enjoying a destination that's happier and more comfortable.

Contrast that with anyone who can't let go of the anger around feeling victimized. People like them don't see anger as a vehicle to effect change. They see anger as the motor home they ride around in all day every day, illegally parking, taking up space in front yards, and sporting bumper stickers like "Honk if you hate everyone!" and "This vehicle speeds up for small children." They use anger as a way to stay boxed into the roles of victim or, sometimes, pariah. They hit and run, squeal their tires, and violate common sense in order to maintain the level of hatred they feel towards the person who caused their anger in the first place.

The conflicts those types of people create in the middle of everyone else's paths are supported and backed up by their giant angry RVs parked sideways across both lanes of emotional traffic. People who live in their anger stand outside the doors of their vehicles, mirrored sunglasses on, arms crossed, and say, "Go back to your life and behave. You can't get past me. You can't win!" Their anger is their identity and they seem unwilling or unable to imagine a life without it.

Much of the time, these perpetually angry people thrive on control and have no trouble using anger to maintain it. Their "nos" are loud and clear and usually mean, "No, you won't get away with going against me."

In defense of the real motor home lifestyle, I've often thought about how fun it would be to travel by RV. I've fantasized about taking a great big expandable thing all around the country, seeing my kids and family and natural wonders several months out of the year. But I will always need a home base—a place with a mailbox, some hosta, good neighbors, and stability. I couldn't live in the small world of my motor home forever.

Those people who live in their anger RVs for years and years never get the sense of peace that comes from focusing inward. They barrel along, wreaking havoc and causing anxiety and pain wherever they go.

Lately, I've been trying not to contact the angry people in my life, particularly my ex-husband, unless I absolutely have to. The anger they carry around with them seems to enjoy nothing more than having me draw attention to myself. It's like a beacon calling forth roadblocks and conflict. Fortunately, the control they used to get from exhibiting anger at me has lost a lot of its power over time.

That doesn't mean my ex-husband doesn't still feel it and try to use it to manipulate me into doing what he wants, nor does it mean that I don't hesitate and re-evaluate my decisions quite often. It doesn't mean that I don't have anxiety about challenging my father's view of the world, either. But they don't scare me anymore. I've learned how to get past the roadblocks—whether it's sneaking down an alley or taking a ramp-enabled leap—so I can continue on my way.

As much as I wish all the angry people in our lives would park their anger in a junkyard to discontinue the road rage, I know they won't be able to until they understand that they'd have a lot more energy to be happy if they didn't spend it being mad.

So until then, they can block our garage doors if they must. We can just go out the side—using our own anger briefly and with purpose to get us where we want to go.

Touching the Trees

Chapter Sixteen
Thunder and Silence

Conflict resolution in my personal relationships hasn't been my strong suit, which is probably quite obvious by now. For someone like me who not only loathes conflict but who has struggled against several identities, any sort of argument, disagreement, or potential for painful emotional interaction can be problematic.

In most situations, I try to learn from my mistakes and do things differently the next time around. After all, isn't Einstein's famous definition of insanity "doing the same thing over and over again and expecting a different result"? But when it came to my pattern of interacting with my ex-husband, I had a difficult time choosing sanity.

There's a cyclical rhythm to all of our relationships. During my marriage, my husband and I cycled just like everyone else. There would be times when we felt like best friends who were emotionally connected to each other. Then there would be times, especially when the kids were very little, that we were like roommates. We loved each other but didn't feel "in love" because the sheer effort it took to get through a day didn't leave enough energy for the relationship. Finally, there were the dark times—the times when one or both of us didn't feel like the marriage was worth salvaging.

Once the dark periods became the dominant phase of the relationship cycle, I initiated the divorce. Unfortunately, that started a whole new cycle of storms and calms.

The storm part of the cycle always started like this: I would ask for something little (a bit of breathing room, a piece of personal property, some understanding, help with the kids, etc.) and he would thunder at me like a window-rattling sonic boom. The amount of anger he'd show me was more than what was necessary to knock me off-balance, and served as a warning about trying to ask for something in the future. It felt like I was sticking my hand out a window during a tornado *knowing* it was going to get torn from my arm.

In our case, his blowback always involved money and respect. He felt like he was giving me more money than I was due and that I wasn't giving him any consideration for being such a decent guy. Money and respect, money and respect.

Those storms occurred so often during our mediation and divorce process that the mediator told me, privately, that he (then, my soon-to-be-ex) was emotionally abusive in the way he "negotiated" with me. Time after time, the mediator saw him turn purple with rage, rock back in his chair, and say, "I'm getting screwed in this deal! You're treating me like I'm nothing but your safety net!" Then he saw me give in because I was afraid of fighting back against straight-line winds like those.

As soon as I gave in on whatever issue was at hand and the conflict was avoided, we'd enter a calm period. Sometimes it happened within minutes of my acquiescence. I'd get some breathing room and could fly under his radar for a little while. I'd use that silence to start building back my confidence; I'd have emotional distance from him and gain strength.

However, there was a problem with that mode of operation: Giving in wasn't ever a guarantee that I was free of the storms. The silence was just a reprieve of unpredictable duration that sometimes allowed for a bit of clean-up.

At the worst of it, this cycle of storms and calms could occur multiple times in one day. Even now, a few years later, that cycle still occurs, though much less frequently. I've learned to be much better about donning emotional protection when I anticipate the beginning of a conflict—which is much different than how I used to act, which was to try to avoid the conflict altogether by giving in relatively quickly.

Awhile back I remember feeling good that I hadn't had any blowups with him for several weeks. In fact, I'd stood my ground about some expenses he wanted me to share and felt like I finally had a healthy foundation from which to grow.

I crawled into bed that night thinking I'd put an end to the storm cycle, but when I checked my email (dumb, dumb, dumb) right before turning off my light, there sat an email from him. I didn't think anything about opening it. After all, I felt pretty well girded. No tornados had blown in lately—it was all good.

But here's what I got...an "Oh, by the way, I've done really well financially *since the divorce* so I've been able to do a lot of really nice things to the house. And although you are responsible for at least half of the crap we accumulated in 20 years of marriage, I'm not going to force you to pay for half the dumpster to haul it away.

"I guess I assumed that you would give me some level of credit for being decent through the separation and discarding process. Perhaps I was wrong."

He had stormed my emotional house again to let me know that he thought he was doing me a financial favor and that I wasn't grateful or respectful enough. The cycle re-commenced: Money and respect. Money and respect.

Although I didn't answer the email (my attempt to create silence for myself), I let him get to me that night. I took my eyes off the sky to give myself a little pat on the back and he swept in. And I've done it a dozen times since then too. Any time we have any discussion about money, he assumes a power position and I feel anxious and afraid of the next thunderclap.

It's possible to identify cycles in relationships, but it's particularly important to do so in ones that are imbalanced or unhealthy. Once we learn the cycle, we can determine whether or not we're willing to continue it.

And it *is* possible to stop the cycle if we're willing to fight through our fear and insecurities.

Touching the Trees

Part III.
Showing Up

Chapter Seventeen
The Replacement

    Here are some interesting coincidences: I'm the oldest child and so is my ex-husband. I have one brother, two sisters; he has one sister, two brothers. Our families' birth orders are the same: girl, boy, girl, girl for me – boy, girl, boy, boy for him. My brother and his sister are both left-handed.

    My mom is from a big farm family; so is his dad. They are also both left-handed. My dad is an only child; so is his mom. They are both right-handed.

    Is that strange enough yet?

Did I mention that his dad looks like old pictures I have of my paternal grandfather?

About a month before I moved out, I began developing feelings for another man. At about that same time, my husband started dating someone else.

Even our post-divorce social life is creepily similar. But I'm working really hard to make sure my similar is actually a well-considered *better*.

A couple of years ago my nearly 19-year-old cat, one that I'd had since he was a kitten, died.

This cat of mine, named Gadget, led a happy full life—if it's possible to determine the quality of a cat's life. He moved eight times, outlived or outlasted two other cats and a dog, sniffed but didn't smother three children, got lost, was found, spent some time high on catnip, and incited riots of hives in my allergic friends. When he finally quit caring what he looked like, he let himself go and sported the cat version of dreadlocks. Waddling with him everywhere he went were impenetrable clumps of fur and dander, making him look more substantial in his wasted body than he really was.

During his last year, I began sometimes taking scissors to his clumps while he patiently, although with some noticeable disdain, sat in my lap. Short of a shaving (and maybe not even then), there was no way he'd ever regain the sleek handsomeness of his middle years, but I felt better knowing that he looked like someone was at least thinking about taking care of him.

Touching the Trees

The end came without warning. On Martin Luther King Day, a Monday night, I was sitting on the floor of my daughter's room reading a book and waiting for her to fall asleep. Shortly after ten I was summoned to the kitchen. My husband pointed down. There on the floor, trying to make his way to the rug in front of the sink, was Gadget. His hind legs were flaccid, his eyes were unfocused, and he was rasping. And yet he tried to pull himself the last few inches to some soft comfort. I guess I shouldn't have been surprised that it was his time. Not his time to go to the vet to be healed, of course, but His Time.

We decided to get the kids out of bed to say goodbye. During the twenty minutes we all sat on the kitchen floor—me cradling Gadget in a towel, the kids rubbing his head and crying—the poor old cat declined to the point where his breaths were coming further and further apart, his tongue was sticking out, and his eyes were fixed and glazed. Worried that the kids would see him actually die, and not quite ready for that, I told their dad he needed to take him to the vet.

After they left, the kids made nests of blankets and pillows in the family room so they could all sleep together. Tears still fell, but we talked about our favorite memories of him (since he was so old and they were young, theirs consisted of things like: "I liked that he slept on my bed." "He never bit me.") Not ten minutes later I got a text. Gadget hadn't made it to the vet. He'd died about a mile away from the house.

That night was hard for the kids. This was their first close brush with death—the great-grandmothers that had passed away in the last few years hadn't been nearly the fixtures in their lives as that scraggly mouser was. The boys wanted to stay home from school. My daughter wanted to know if she could have a snack. Their dad, when he finally came home, wanted to mourn in private and go to bed.

Then six days later, before Gadget's ashes were even back from the vet, we adopted two new kittens.

I caught a lot of grief for getting new kittens. Not from the kids, of course, but from nearly everyone else.

My daughter's friend said, "You're supposed to wait six months like we did."

Zane said, "It's okay for the kids to be sad for a while. You know, it's also okay for *you* to be sad for a while."

Maybe they were right. Maybe it's not always good to get new when you've just lost old. But I felt compelled to replace him, quickly and with something busy and joyful, especially since I knew that the end of my marriage was close at hand.

I thought about the ends of relationships. They are chaotic, full of anguish and self-doubt. There are some moments when homicide (or at least some horrific accident) seems both necessary and justifiable. There are other moments when it's easier to curl up on yourself, sobbing into your knees, than it is to think five minutes into the future. Still other moments disappear, lost in the numbness of reordering your world. And all of those reactions occur, sometimes in the same day, because there's a giant void in your life where the relationship used to be. You may hate your former partner, but you miss that recognizable life.

I didn't hate Gadget, of course, but I did miss having cat fur on the couch, if you can believe that.

I bet you could read ten books about divorce and every one of them would say that you shouldn't get into a serious relationship right after your marriage ends. (I know you can, actually, because I've read them.) They offer psychological explanations for why you can't trust your instincts at that point in your life and they warn of inevitable second breakups. They cite statistics that couldn't possibly lie. You'll be sorry, they portend. You'll be sorrier and lonelier than you are right now if you screw up and hop on the first relationship that comes your way.

Those books are probably right, if what you're doing is filling a void. If the person you've found is a replacement. If you haven't done what you need to do—understand your motivations, your weaknesses, your desires, and your patterns of behavior—and changed what needed to be changed.

We've all seen it. The rebound relationship fills the empty chair where the cat used to lie.

My ex-husband has probably fallen prey to that. I'm not sure my bags were even packed before he "reconnected" with a woman he hadn't seen after their brief professional relationship ended several years before. What I am sure of, though, is that he still told me he loved me and offered me chances to stay. So which was it? He fought me with everything in his arsenal to keep me from leaving, including long manipulations about how I was doing irreparable damage to the kids. And yet, before I even moved out, he'd begun to replace me.

I met my replacement. I wanted to. It was a condition I set with my ex-husband before he could introduce her to my kids. I was also curious to see this woman who supposedly looked just like me (she kind of does). What struck me during our conversation (besides the fact that she was drinking water, which, combined with her age, made me unfairly question her pregnancy status) was that she was a lot like me, except that she was also a bit of who I *wanted* to be. She was a bit of that person I was seeking in myself.

She was independent, divorced, and able to survive on her own. She was employed as a professional and had so much disposable income that she owned two cars—one a convertible luxury car. She'd found herself, it appeared, and I was still stumbling around on the journey. He'd replaced me, all right. With a five-years-from-now-yet-younger version of me. A life-sized cliché.

Finding a replacement is my default setting too, though. I replaced my alpha-male, controlling father with an alpha-male, controlling husband. A couple of years ago I contemplated replacing my alpha-male controlling husband with that guy I met at the bar. He was a lot like my husband but different enough to make him temporarily attractive. I wish I could remember when I realized that he was a replacement, but I can't. I just sensed that both men were cut from the same self-focused, ladder-climbing, wife-ignoring cloth.

I wasn't seeing Zane at the time I met that guy, but I sure knew what I didn't want. I didn't want to make another mistake. Without the saving grace of that tiny bit of self-awareness, I might have replaced. And I, too, might have replaced before my bags were even packed.

To avoid the replacement partner, you have to want to do something different. Not only do you have to want it, though, you need to work at it. The first step is to understand that it's easy to fill the void where the marriage or relationship used to be with someone that appears to have your ex's good qualities and none of his or her bad. In the guy at the bar, I first saw a professionally successful, financially secure, socially confident man who was willing and able to appreciate a smart woman. He was my default and my radar picked up on that. Once you understand your own default—the type of person you gravitate to—you'll be alert, too.

The second step in avoiding the possibly-doomed replacement partner is to define what you want in a relationship. I don't know how I've managed to hold on to that list of twelve things I want in a partner, but it's been helpful in keeping me focused on what I want from a relationship. While that may seem a little structured, especially for someone like me who loses car keys unless I leave them in the car, it's been a great tool to keep me on a road that leads away from the replacement and, hopefully, toward fulfillment.

I don't believe you have to avoid any new beginnings right after your breakup—you just have to be conscious and wary. Because, chances are your default setting feels like a really safe place to land and you'll go there if there don't seem to be any alternatives. In other words, although two fluffy mewling kittens seem like a great idea, they'll get matted and old just like the last one did.

So try something different. First try living with the void for a while. Then maybe get a dog.

Touching the Trees

Chapter Eighteen
Worlds Colliding

This seems like an excellent time to introduce you to Peter.

Me, I met him a few years ago at a Christmas party. He remembers that we met in the kitchen. I remember meeting in the dining room. It doesn't matter, really.

What matters is that he, my husband, and I became casual friends, running into each other occasionally at neighborhood parties, backyard bonfires, and sometimes driving down the street.

What also matters is that he was the least flirtatious man I'd ever met. Yet, I found myself seeking out his eye contact, or gravitating toward where he was sitting, or developing a need for a next beer when he was up getting his own.

Just from watching him around our friends and his son, I fell into a significant fantasy crush that was secret and unrequited. Remember how I could be happy for hours after making eye contact with a stranger at a stop light? A night spent at the same gathering as Peter was the same kind of tide-over. After all, I was married (albeit lonely) and his neighbor, which meant that any relationship beyond the pretend one in my head was off-limits.

He made it easy to keep my thoughts hidden, then, because he didn't seem to notice me any more than he noticed any of the other neighborhood women. I didn't think he caught me watching him or coincidentally joining his conversations.

But it turns out he did.

Shortly after leaving my marriage, I began living in two worlds. The first one was reality. It was where I took care of my kids just like I always did, worked for the first time in fifteen years, hung out with the friends I've had for years, and spent considerable amounts of phone time with a couple of my siblings. It was also the place where I was in charge of a large volunteer organization and a member of a couple of other ones, one national and one local. Reality was where I knew my boxes and I was reasonably comfortable with my identity as a single woman. I was a mom, a friend, a sister, a daughter, an ex-wife, and a know-it-all volunteer.

Fantasy was where I lived alone (when my kids were with their dad) in the house of my own choosing, spent time talking to and expanding my friendship with Peter, rode on the back of a motorcycle, and wrote.

At the onset of fantasy, right after I moved out, I did almost all I could to keep those worlds from colliding. I didn't want anyone in my "real life" to know I was hanging out with Peter because I thought it reflected badly on my stated desire for independence. I thought it looked like I was the cheater I'd been so diligent about not becoming.

On the other hand, fantasy was the only safe place where I could escape to break down, throw my head back and laugh, or sit for hours and write about nothing and everything. I felt safe in that world, safe to hold his hand or lounge on a couch with him talking about our pasts, our dreams, our kids, and our families. My secret crush wasn't unrequited anymore, but I still wanted to keep it to myself.

One problem with that, though, was that Peter was part of my reality before we started dating. A lot of our early time together was taken up trying to analyze and strategize how to keep our relationship from encroaching on my ex-husband's and joint friends' lives so that no one felt uncomfortable. Together and separately,

Touching the Trees

Peter and I probably spent more time making sure everyone else was okay with our relationship than we did making sure *we* were okay with it. Certainly, we put more effort into making other people feel good about us than we needed to.

At the time, however, we felt like we had good reason to think so carefully about the situation. There were a few truths that we couldn't deny. One was that I sought a divorce partly because I *did* want to be independent. I *did* want to go it alone and do it all myself. I wanted to prove to myself that I didn't need anyone, least of all another man, to take care of me and my children financially, physically, or emotionally.

Another truth was that my children were going through a lot of transition, turmoil, and emotional whiplash and I didn't want to take any attention away from making sure they were doing okay during the divorce period. They deserved to have all of me when they were in my care and I believed it would be easier for them if they didn't think their mom was jumping into something new, like their dad was, that would detract from them.

A third truth was that there were a few other people, in addition to my ex-husband, who weren't happy that we were together. My ex—well, he already had a girlfriend that he'd been trotting around since before I moved out, but he'd be damned if he'd "lose" to the guy across the street. For a while, anytime I saw him he'd begin a new tirade of slurs and threats of financial retribution, simply because he was so angry at me for dating Peter.

Neighbors were put out because "neighborhood harmony" was wrecked as a result of our relationship. What had once been a close-knit community of neighbor-friends was divided because both my ex-husband and Peter still lived there. People weren't sure who to side with—the guy they felt sorry for because his wife left him or the guy who'd been their friend longer.

Close friends of mine were cautious at best because they didn't want me to leap into another man's control and make the same mistakes I'd been making. While they all liked Peter a lot, they were concerned that I wasn't working hard enough on myself, resetting my defaults.

So Peter and I chose to keep our private life together quiet and segregated from reality.

Little by little, though, we poked at other peoples' discomfort with a long stick and watched to see if any bears awoke: I took Peter to a party of some old friends. He introduced me to his mom when she was in town. After six months, I told my kids I'd gone on a couple of dates with him. The neighbors started to accept us, for the most part, and tried not to act any differently around us. I introduced him to some extended family and he introduced me to some high school friends. With the exception of any interaction with my ex-husband, the encounters went smoothly.

For some time now, Peter and I have been part of each other's lives and have worked very hard on our relationship—maintaining honesty and respect, giving without conditions, and making memories. Although we haven't sought to label or define our relationship, we have built a little superfamily that's felt good to us.

But there were some arenas where our worlds didn't collide for a long time. My reality of sitting on the sidelines or in the audience, cheering my kids on and chatting with other parents, was Peter-free for months and months. My reality of the daily grind—carpooling, laundry, dishes, vacuuming, and all other things domestic—also stayed rather Peter-free for at least that long.

I struggled with if, when, and how to fully combine my life with Peter's. When I watched my kids play sports and I sat within feet of my ex-husband's girlfriend—the woman who would be the next me, the one who discounted my parenting, and who encouraged my ex to change his hairstyle into something suspiciously GQ, I wanted nothing more than for Peter to be there with me, propping me up, reminding me that I was worthy of love and respect. I wanted to bring Peter into the fold and show him this real life that I led without him—the one where I was a proud mother and a biggest fan.

Mostly, though, I didn't want to give my ex-husband, friends, or fears power over me anymore. I'd given my ex control over my decisions, my identity, and my emotions during the marriage. Then, when there was no marriage, I still gave him control in my relationship with Peter—by continuing to fear his reactions and by keeping my two worlds from colliding.

Over cups of coffee or glasses of wine, I talked with my friends and explained to them that I wanted Peter in my life because he was respectful of my needs and willing to be patient as I strived for a newer, stronger identity. Rather than stealing my independence, Peter actually applauded it.

As for my fears—those were a little harder to grasp and tame. I was still afraid that I was jumping into a relationship too early. I was still fearful that I would make a mistake that would be costly to my kids, to Peter, and to my self-esteem.

Finally, though, I understood that fear—in this case, fear that my world without Peter and my world with Peter would collide and explode— was just another way of not trusting my decisions. It was another way of keeping me dependent on the ways of my past.

Touching the Trees

Chapter Nineteen
The Tent Caterpillar

It comes as no surprise, especially to my male friends, that my ex-husband hates Peter viscerally and with a passion that is not abating.

I have a tougher time understanding. The logic I work under is this:

1. My ex is still in a committed relationship and his girlfriend seems to be doing a great job of occupying his time and attention.
2. He got everything he wanted—the house, the amount of custody, the money settlements, etc.

3. He knew Peter as long and, for a while, as well as I did. And liked him.
4. He knows I didn't have an affair.
5. We're *divorced*.

So he should get over it already, right?

But here's the problem. That hate, the hate that's as much an entity in our current situation as the marriage once was, is destructive. This is not only true for my ex-husband, who is surely suffering from the inside out, but for me—because I have let it eat at me too.

Zane told me once that every time I engaged in dialogue or discussion with my ex about trigger topics (money, the kids, or Peter) I was painting a bulls-eye on myself and running at the poison-tipped arrow.

He wasn't far off, except that I wasn't running anywhere. I was standing still, frozen to one spot, and letting it happen. Where was that new woman I wanted to be? Where was my independence and fortitude? Why wasn't I able to achieve freedom from the role I used to play?

Recently, on a trip to rural western Wisconsin, I saw young trees on the side of the road, some growing out of ditches and some lining the edges of horse pastures or soybean fields. A handful of these saplings hosted white web pouches that were positioned where a branch sprouted off from the main trunk. Even in brief glimpses, I could see a grayish mass toward the center interior of each pouch. Had I pulled over and gotten out to investigate further, I would have seen that the gray mass was dozens of tent caterpillars wriggling in the afternoon sunlight.

The tent caterpillar is an interesting creature. Not nearly as destructive as the webworm, which builds massive multiple webs and can devastate whole tree farms or forests, the tent caterpillar's damage can be undone by the next growing season if the population is controlled properly. But it does cause damage. It's a pest.

During this trip to Wisconsin, I tried to stay engaged in my journey, appreciating wild columbine and breathing in the roadside lilac. I had deep conversation with my traveling companions and ate at a fabulous diner that looked suspiciously like a suped-up funeral home. It was a beautiful, sunny day—nearly perfect by all measurable standards. But just when I would lose myself in the unexpected sight of a well-groomed horse nibbling grass by a stream in the middle of nowhere or an old couple sitting on a front porch waving at the visitors passing through town, my mind would drift away. I would think about my ex-husband and how he inserted himself into my life in ways I wish I could control better and in places I wish he would stay out of for good. Like the tent caterpillar, he was a pest.

Ever since the divorce, that man has been the third wheel when I've gone on dates to the movies, crunching popcorn in my ear and frowning when I laugh too loudly in a quiet theater. He's positioned himself on the center of a motorcycle, leaning into me to keep me from leaning into the driver. He's sat in my office tapping keys to cause misspellings, and he's found me in the women's room of a nice restaurant to remind me that, while dinner may have been delicious and my date finds me attractive, my breath smells like garlic. He's shown up at a small gathering of close friends late at night, jerking his chin toward the door and challenging me to defy him by staying. He's been in bed with me a handful of times when I've been in bed with someone else, shielding his eyes from my stretch-marked stomach and becoming angry that the pleasure I feel isn't one that I felt with him.

He's rarely actually anywhere near me, of course, yet he's often there anyway, building tents where there should only be growth and gnawing on my tender new leaves until I feel raw and exposed. What I haven't found yet, but soon need to, is a way to scrape those tents from their moorings.

The tent caterpillars need warmth and sun to survive and aid digestion of leaf buds. My ex-husband needed an emotional response from me. Tent caterpillars find sunny tree crotches to build their homes; he would find the places that make me happy and take up residency there. While the caterpillars leave pheromone trails as they enter and exit the tent to forage and sleep, he left stinging barbs to make sure I noticed his comings and goings.

Tent caterpillars are also a feast-or-famine species. When they've found an area that can support a population, they send out chemical signals that attract more of their kind. Very quickly, the numbers of hungry, marauding caterpillars expand exponentially, causing increasingly more damage.

Like them, when my ex-husband realized that he'd found particularly charged situations, like my children's sporting events or the final disposition of twenty years of goods and memories, he'd begin chewing on me relentlessly until I was reduced to a pulpy confused mess. When I would finally walk away, he would stand erect, smiling, bits and pieces of my tenderness stuck to his face. It was then, when he'd had his fill—when he'd leeched enough out of me to feed his resentment and anger—that he would leave me alone for a while so I could attempt to re-grow what he'd destroyed. He damaged me for a long time.

Unfortunately, this behavior of his didn't just show up after we were divorced, which is why I couldn't stay married to him. But it keeps happening, even now that the marriage is over and he's moved on to another relationship. He isn't about live and let live. He's about getting what he wants and ignoring the pain he causes in the process. He always has been and, I believe, he always will be.

I've done a lot of work trying to rid myself of his parasitic bite-marks. I've re-learned how to trust other people; I've allowed myself to feel loved. I've decided to accept the parts of me that I dislike, but that are unchangeable (like those stretch marks). I've moved on, forward and upward. But I still have a weakness that he can exploit. It's my need to be happy and at peace.

See, while that need should be a positive thing, it's the conditions that go into that joy and contentment that expose me to him. He knows that I'm incapable of feeling good about myself if I'm closed off from the people and situations that I care about—like my kids, my friends, my gardens, my writing. So when I'm open and welcoming to all of those people and things, I don't have a quick enough shut-off valve when he decides to invade. So he does.

By doing a little research, I found there are several ways to eliminate the tent caterpillar. Most exotically, you can get a cuckoo bird, which is its natural predator. Or you can find a long stick, rip open the sac and allow the caterpillars to spill to the ground, where you'll need to crunch them under your work boots, spray them with poison, or torch them with fire. You can even let them eat everything in sight until there is no more sustenance and they starve themselves to death or move on.

I could do all of those types of things, too, with the exception of getting a cuckoo bird. I could harass my ex-husband, cause him legal trouble, turn his children against him, or isolate him from his so-called friends. Or, I could continue to let him have access to the best of me until there's nothing left and he moves on to someone else.

But what I've learned is that the most effective method of eradicating tent caterpillars is to fill a bucket a quarter of the way up with water and set it near the tent caterpillars' tree, preferably on the pheromone path they usually take in and out of their webs. They will march deliberately up and over the lid of the bucket and they'll drown.

For those of us with parasitic relationships that we have trouble controlling, the equivalent of a drowning-bucket needs to be our silence. We need to keep those people that will feed on our weaknesses in the cruel shade of unknowing. We need to starve them of our attention and our emotional power. We can do this by not responding to phone calls, emails, or verbal confrontations unless absolutely necessary. For me, it means setting limits to what I'll discuss and being willing to walk out on a conversation or refuse to return a phone call if he crosses my boundaries.

Since our "tent caterpillars" will be no better able to adapt to being cut off from us than the real tent caterpillars are able to sprout fins and gills, their power over us will die.

Our leaves—our strength—will grow back.

Touching the Trees

Chapter Twenty
My Hero-Worshipping Moth

Speaking of caterpillars—although not ones that will destroy everything in our paths—one of the first lifecycles kids are exposed to is "a caterpillar can become a beautiful butterfly." I'm still amazed that a crusty silk cocoon can provide an environment of such transformational magnitude.

Left to my own devices, I would watch that whole process from start to finish. I wouldn't even care if the creature that emerged at the end was a monarch or a common brown moth. It would be amazing because of its journey. At this point in my life I'm fond of journeys.

When my children were born I quickly figured out that I wasn't in a category of parents who consider children to be possessions. From the get-go I believed that my kids were mine on loan—that my responsibility was to raise them to be strong, capable, empathetic, contributing participants in their own life paths. I didn't believe, nor do I now, that I owned them or that I should feel compelled to control every aspect of their lives. I was and am still a cocoon, but I won't be forever. Part of my role as their mother is to understand my children so I can guide them; part of my role as a single mother is to give them tools to have a good relationship with their dad.

One of my kid's animal kingdom alter-ego is the moth. This kid of mine has the empathic abilities of Deanna Troi (air-fives to my Trekkie friends) mixed with the hero worship of the firefly. Even though he can feel the emotional static, he can't help being drawn to a pretty, blinding light.

I've always loved his sensitivity—even as a toddler, he instinctively knew to pick up his baby brother's pacifier off the ground, lick off the fuzz (ok, he learned that from me), and squirt it back into the baby's mouth before he began to fuss. He was the kid that always told me everything would be all right, right after I had a grown-up temper tantrum. He was the one that seemed to handle the divorce the best—and I believed it was because he could finally feel at ease, at least half the time. But he was also the one that said, "Who's going to protect us now, Mom, now that you're not there anymore?"

He's my heartacher and the apple that didn't far fall from my late-blooming tree.

Which is why we are able to talk openly about his relationship with his dad, even if it's sometimes hard for me to maintain my resolve to be a guide and not a driver.

For a long time, I've worried that my Moth and his dad were destined for issues. Moth has always been able to understand his dad's justifications and defenses when he misses a milestone event, but continues to crave his approval and attention anyway. It's like Troi meets the bug zapper. But now that Moth and his dad are together without me as a buffer, he struggles with how to communicate his needs and concerns. He doesn't want to "make the situation worse" by confronting his dad when he's frustrated, but he's starting to let his own needs take a back seat to that caretaking.

The night he first told me his fears about talking to his dad, I wanted to raise my hands to the sky and say, "That, my boy, is precisely why I'm not married to the man anymore." His dad doesn't take well to being questioned and he has an even harder time making long-term behavioral changes.

During that conversation, Moth said he felt like his dad was more interested in hanging out with his girlfriend than the kids. Moth worried that his dad's minor legal trouble was signaling a downward spiral. He was incredibly hurt that his dad has spent thousands of dollars redecorating the house but that he didn't see that erasing me from the house also erased parts of the kids. Like me, Moth missed the play figures with his name written, in permanent marker (ala Toy Story), on the soles of their oversized boots. Unlike me, he had to see them at the bottom of a dumpster, poking out from under pounds and boxes of other memories.

This kid needs his dad, just like I needed a husband. But he's afraid to reach out and ask for what he needs, already. Just like I was, forever.

In that conversation that night, I asked Moth to picture what he wanted his relationship with his dad to look like. Did he want someone to watch television with, attend games with, or go hunting or fishing with? Or did he want someone who could put aside his own "stuff", whether it was work or the girlfriend or the laundry, and just hang out?

I told him to give that some thought. Then I asked him how he wanted to share that information with his dad. Did he want to write him a letter? (I told him that his dad was quite used to getting letters, since that had always been the best way for me to communicate with him.) Did he want to schedule some time to talk with him? Did he want me to help facilitate that?

Then—and this may not have been the right thing to talk with my son about—I told him that I, too, was concerned about his dad. I also told him that I couldn't be the one to take care of his dad anymore. *Nor was that **his** job.* His dad needed to learn how to take care of himself.

Earlier that day, as part of a discussion my boys and I had about the effects of divorce on the future marriages of kids, it came up that one of the risk factors for divorce is marrying too young. I told them that I felt like being too young was a contributing factor to my own divorce. Because they're smart, one of them said, "So, are you saying this is the first time you've ever lived on your own?" Yes, I was saying that.

So later, as Moth and I were discussing his dad, I told him that 1) his dad didn't do me any favors by taking care of the finances all those years—I didn't learn what I needed to about financially running a household until the embarrassing age of 42 (and at that point I hadn't gone through an entire tax year yet, so the jury was still a little bit out on whether I really could). I also told him that 2) I didn't do his dad any favors by always taking care of him emotionally and socially. As hard as it was for him to see his dad fail or be upset, it was an important thing for his dad to go through and learn from.

My Moth gets it. But he still craves his dad's approval and love. Of course, I give him all the love I can and I always have. He knows he can talk to me; he knows I'm safe, even when I'm ranting about chores or food wrappers. He knows I love him unconditionally—somewhere deep inside, I bet he even remembers that I was always the one to hold him and say, "Let it out, honey. You'll be okay." But I also know he wishes his dad could have said the same thing, instead of yelling at him to stop crying.

I want my children to have a good relationship with their dad—one that can be a model for their own parenthood someday. I just wish they didn't have to work through the same haze of fear and anxiety that I had to. When I embarked on my journey to a more authentic life, I didn't realize that I'd already laid the groundwork for at least one of my children to follow in the footsteps I didn't mean to leave behind. Now it's my job to help him step onto a different path.

I hope that someday soon my son will get the courage to reach out to his dad. And when that day comes, I hope the bug zapper is off and his dad's defenses are on low power. A moth that beautiful deserves at least that much from his hero.

Chapter Twenty-One
Hanging Light Fixtures

Sometimes I feel like asking for help means I'm incapable. And one thing I really don't want to believe about myself is that I'm incapable, so I don't like to ask for help.

The women I most greatly admire are the ones that do it all on their own—raise families, have careers, move furniture, fix sinks, and create their own happiness—without dependence on a man.

That is not to say that I'm in any way a man-hater; quite the opposite. It's just that I've gone through most of my adulthood having to confer with or acquiesce to a couple of strong-willed men and I'm often in awe of women who haven't.

When I bought my new house after the divorce, I was fairly sure I could do anything I needed to to take care of it. I could shimmy up the ladder and clean gutters (or, better yet, have my kids do it). I could change the kitchen faucet, light the water heater's pilot light, and paint bedrooms. I could even arrange and rearrange furniture in the ways that made the most sense to me.

But one thing I *couldn't* do was change out the obtrusive brass candelabra hanging in my dining room in time for my housewarming party. And, man, did I want to. However, not only did I not have one ounce of knowledge about or interest in working with electricity, I didn't have enough arm or ladder length to reach the vaulted ceiling.

So I had to do the thing I didn't want to do. I had to ask for help.

Peter agreed to work on it for me.

It was kind of a good deal for me because I did have some part in the installation—I turned breaker switches off and on (this was where my limited working knowledge of electrical came in handy), pointed a flashlight, and stabilized the old and new light fixtures on their way down and up. I also taught my daughter how to plunk "Yankee Doodle" on my out-of-tune piano during the process, and it became the sound track for Hanging the Light Fixture, over and over and over.

"Yankee Doodle came to town, riding on a pony…"

I hadn't seen Peter work on a project before and I enjoyed watching his process. First, he laid out the parts to be installed. There were neat piles of screws, chain, wire, etc. Then he quickly disassembled the old fixture and lowered it to me on the ground. Finally, he started work on the new one. Occasionally he would stop, read the directions, hold a part in his hand, and examine it closely. Then he would climb the ladder again and proceed.

Within about 45 minutes and 30 verses of theme song, Peter erected the new fixture—more wrought iron-esque and modern— and asked me to flip the breaker switches a few more times before pronouncing the fixture installed. The only thing that didn't work was the dimmer, but he determined that it was a house wiring issue instead of a fixture issue. He also said he had an extra dimmer at home that he could install later, if I wanted. Well, sure, that sounded great if I couldn't figure out how to do it myself.

"Stuck a feather in his hat and called it macaroni…"

After the ladder was removed, the table under the light replaced, and we were enjoying the way the new fixture tied the entire room together, I thanked him for taking care of that for me with only two days to spare before the party.

"No problem," he said. "It was fun. But I should tell you something."

"What?" I asked.

"I've actually never done that before."

"Really?"

"Yeah. I thought it would be fun to figure out how to do it. So I did it."

Huh, I thought. How nice it must be to see a problem, know that you have the skills to figure it out, and actually solve it—even with the pressure of a hovering deadline.

Which got me thinking: How often do I do that? And more importantly, how often have I been too afraid to try?

"Hanging a light fixture" has become Peter's and my catch phrase for trying something new. But it really should be a way of living. Feeling a sense of security that I can survive through problem-solving? How wonderful would that be?

There have been plenty of chances for me to hang light fixtures in the last few years. The processes of deciding to divorce, really leaving, buying a house, moving twice, and signing the final papers have all been episodes of hanging light fixtures. But there have been more chances—*are* more chances—that I've been shying away from.

Which has caused me to face some shadowy corners and empty ceilings. And doubt my skills. Do I have what it takes to continue moving forward and not get stuck in some identity that's as wrong for me as the last one? Do I have what it takes to support myself and my children? Do I have what it takes to keep my volunteer endeavors successful? Do I have the motivation to install a light fixture when I'm not at all sure that it will hang straight or turn on?

Then there's my personal life. My post-marriage relationship with Peter has been a light fixture hanging extravaganza. It's all new, even the parts that are a result of pushing away from the old relationship. Each time there's been a choice—whether to share a thought, to tell the whole truth, or to express an emotion—I've had to deliberately choose to do things differently than ever before. And it's been hard.

"Mind the music and the step, and with the girls be handy…"

Every new movement forward we have to take with fresh shoes and clean socks. And we have to trust that we have the skills to create something we've never experienced before. There are a lot of frilly brass candelabras, relics from another time, we can lower to the floor.

Our challenge is to find the confidence to sort through options, assess skills, and take a stab at hanging a fixture, solving a problem, and making a connection that will tie the whole thing together.

Touching the Trees

Chapter Twenty-Two
Base Frequency and the Emotional Doppler Effect (Or, Tuning Forks and Dandelions)

Prior to making so many drastic changes in my life, I was a full-time parent, a full-time volunteer, and a part-time writer. My yearly income from writing was about $400 (which, of course, was $400 more per year than I received from parenting or volunteering). Although I'd been a teacher once, I hadn't worked outside the home in fourteen years and didn't have any credentials in place to begin teaching again once I was divorced.

Like so many newly single women (or, more generally, newly single non-bread-winners), I panicked about needing a full-time job, with benefits, pronto.

My ex-husband perpetuated that panic by emailing me job openings for claims adjusters, telemarketing representatives, and inside sales managers. He reminded me that freedom came with a price and that he wasn't keen on being my financial safety net for the rest of my life.

In reality, part of me was excited about the prospect of wearing work clothes and getting a paycheck. That part of me thought, "Yeah, this is what I want—professional recognition and a *title*." Never mind that my ex was simply trying to reduce his alimony obligation; it was time for me to get a job. A real job.

And, by some kind of miracle, I did.

Music is embedded into me, even though I never became a professional musician. For their entire lives my father's parents were, though—Grandma played viola, piano, and celeste with a metropolitan symphony and Grandpa was always in a big band, toting around a sousaphone. My dad, although he never pursued music as a career, has always played trumpet and piano. When he turned 60, he decided to teach himself French horn. He plays in his Lodge band all year long.

I used to sing into dandelion microphones at the end of the driveway and my sibling troupe would perform dance routines on the fireplace hearth for anyone who would watch. To this day, when I turn off the radio or the iPod, the last song playing is the one that sticks in my head like a broken record until I hear something new.

When I was a kid, raised in an environment where I was more likely to hum Rimsky-Korsakov or Stan Kenton than current pop stars (a few years ago I found out that my mom still wasn't quite sure who the Beatles were), my two favorite items were the tuning fork and the metronome. I loved the magic of the tuning fork's two prongs that sang out a pure note if they were tapped on a table or a knee. I knew that if I could get my violin's A string to synchronize with the tuning fork's A, the rest of my strings would eventually be in tune too.

Our metronome was pyramidal polished wood and steadied my tendency to rush through the easy parts and to slow down on the hard notes. Even now I can hear that old taskmaster clicking 60 beats per minute, its metal weight swinging back and forth like a trapeze artist. (Having long-since retired and become imbalanced, the metronome now occupies a place of honor in my living room.)

My son said something interesting to me the one day, which got me thinking about those old musical helpers, especially the tuning fork. We were in the car and he shook his head, twice, like he was getting his bangs out of his eyes. Then he said, "I just heard my base frequency."

I asked him what that meant. He explained, "A base frequency is that hum you can sometimes hear in your ears. It's when your body becomes in tune with itself for a few seconds."

Huh. I should mention here that he's not a student of philosophy or of biophysics. At the time, he was a fourteen-year-old boy who loved to make me cringe by pulling open his sleeve and showing me his armpit hair.

But what if he was right, despite his unfolding puberty and requisite goofiness? What if every once in a while our bodies "true-up" and we get back to our base frequency? What if, somewhere in our inner self, there's a tiny little tuning fork that emits a pure tone when all the atoms around it align into our own distinct, individual pattern? And...what if intuition is the guide we use to get back to our base frequency?

In the last couple of years I haven't heard any ringing in my ears (thankfully), but I've learned to trust my intuition more than I ever have before. Also, I can feel when I'm getting out of emotional alignment and can do a gut-check—which is essential, I think, to moving forward on a path of "yeses" rather than backwards or sideways when I run into those "nos."

When I was married, though, I rarely re-tuned myself. Mostly I ignored the parts of me that were out of whack and let someone else's frequency determine my own. Frankly, I didn't trust that my tuning fork hadn't gone rusty from too little sleep and too much stress.

Then came a really big test of my intuition. Shortly after I left my husband, when I was in the throes of uncertainty, I took a full-time job in Human Resources. At that point in my life I had no business training, no experience, and certainly no knowledge of benefits and worker's compensation. All I had, which is what landed me the interview and subsequently the job, were the skills I'd learned as a volunteer. Read: I could talk, listen, problem solve, and mediate—even with adults, not just with my kids. Plus I knew the owner of the company, although I'm quite certain he didn't just gift me the position (mostly because he was good friends with my ex-husband).

As several people will attest, I felt that job coming toward me. A couple of months before it materialized, I went out on a limb and told Zane and a few close friends that I knew something good was heading down the pike. As sure as a person can hear a semi-truck speed by on the highway or a helicopter zip through the sky, I could hear a distant whine of something big that had me in its sights. I could also feel that job make a wave in my world, like a penny plopped into a lake. The ensuing ripples got closer and closer and finally the job became a reality.

Somehow my base frequency picked up all those changes in pressure. I don't generally believe that intuition has the powers of a crystal ball-reading gypsy, but in those months before the job was even created (it was a brand-new position for that company), I felt at peace knowing that everything would work out soon.

As you might remember from middle school science, the Doppler Effect is when you can hear something coming at one pitch, hear the pitch lower and stabilize as it passes you, and hear it go down even lower as it speeds away. It's the three different notes sirens and race cars make as they approach, pass, and leave. It's the explanation for why the same engine can make different sounds as it travels and why, in the physical world, waves get closer together at the shoreline.

In terms of our base frequency, it's also what happens when we run into situations and people as they pass through our daily lives. Anticipation often causes more disturbance (excitement, anxiety, dread, fear) than actuality does. Think of a roller coaster ride or a blind date—the most terrifying part is when you're climbing the big hill or sitting at the bar alone. The emotional Doppler Effect is at work.

My job followed that same pattern. It was high-pitched excitement and anxiety as it approached. The salary was more than I'd ever made in my life; it was the stable, yet flexible, full-time job I needed to be able to buy a house and take care of my kids; and my lack of experience seemed to be less important to the company than my natural abilities. It was also a drastic lifestyle change coming on the heels of several other drastic lifestyle changes. Overall, though, it seemed perfect and, frankly, a gift from heaven.

I needed that job—needed it to boost my self-esteem, needed it to distract me from the pain of divorcing, and needed it in order to prove that *I had what it takes*. And as my first day of work approached, that job did all those things for me. I felt great about the idea of working and rather enjoyed the run-up to day one, despite a lack of appetite and innumerable outfit changes.

The true pitch of a sound can only be heard when neither the source of the sound is moving, nor is the listener. It's like the tuning fork—the person holding it can't wander around the stage while everyone tunes their instruments or the pitches will be off.

I finally got to hear the true pitch of that job once I started there. Unfortunately, it didn't gel with my own base frequency—at all. Even remotely. In fact, it was so bad that it was like playing, simultaneously, two notes that are next to each other in a scale. They clash, they sound awful, and (if you listen carefully) they cause a rhythmic thumping as their sound waves bump into each other. As the immortalized Sesame Street song goes, "One of these things is not like the other…." I didn't fit there and couldn't seem to figure out how to change my base frequency so that I would get along better.

Then I realized I didn't want to.

To this day, I can't put my finger on exactly how my heaven-sent job went so wrong so quickly. There were personality conflicts, sure, but I'd maneuvered through those before, when I was a teacher and while volunteering. And part of why they hired me was that I could do that very thing. But in that office there was undermining and back-stabbing in quantities and varieties I'd never seen before. There was even one particular incident that bordered, rather closely, on sexual harassment.

I don't mean to pat myself on the back here, but I can count on very few fingers how many people I haven't been able to get along with (okay, that might simply be because I hate conflict). There were two in that ten person office alone. I rubbed them very wrongly all the time and vice-versa. In short, it was miserable in fewer than three days. When I went to work every day after that, I could hear our frequencies bumping into each other in a really bad way. Thump. Thump. Thump.

But I stayed, bought a house, managed a second move in four months, and did my best to keep my kids okay.

Then one weekend I just listened.

I listened to my intuition (at the time it manifested itself as a very anxious stomach) and its off-tune, out-of-rhythm lament. I felt the waves of discontent crash into my side as I contemplated a future at that company. The beating I'd heard before was from contradictory notes, but added to that was a different rhythm—the beating of my own heart rebelling against that whole situation.

Exactly three months after I stepped into the tall brown pumps of Human Resources Director, I got a newly-constructed office, complete with a window, brand-new furniture, and paint fumes. On that same day, I resigned.

My base frequency hummed.

I know I was lucky to have the option to resign. I know there are thousands upon thousands of women and men who have to put up with the deafening "whump, whump" of knowing they're in an unhealthy situation and believing they can't get out. I know that, in desperation, people will do anything to escape their own pain. They will also put up with anything to take care of their children. I do know I was lucky, believe me.

But what happened to my intuition at the beginning? What happened to the premonition that something fantastic was going to happen and I'd be okay? How could I have been so wrong about the big thing coming towards me?

Here's how…because the job wasn't the big thing coming towards me, after all. *It was the life after the job.* Removing my financial safety net was a bit of a crazy move, yes. But that job had become a metaphor for the marriage I'd just left. All the same patterns were in play—all the same manipulations and power-struggles, thumping and clashing. And I wasn't going to go through that again. I wasn't going to waste the opportunities I'd created for myself as a result of the divorce by stuffing them into a headache-inducing office, filling out county assistance forms for employees, and listening to webinars on wage-an-hour issues.

As I told my employer on the day I resigned: I'm not a quitter. However, that position was leading me to quit on myself—to give up my dreams and my passions just so I could slog through day after day of political sucker punches and cold-cocks to my integrity. So, by resigning, I was actually choosing to keep going on the path I both wanted and needed to take. The path I was destined to take. This one, right here.

To move forward through transitions, we have to listen very carefully to our unease. The nervousness, stomachaches, headaches, and restlessness all tell us that when we need to change directions. They are our Doppler Effects.

It's *how* we decide to change directions that allows our base frequency to align itself. When we make choices that are right for us, whether it's to take a new job, recommit to a relationship, or step back from an unhealthy situation, our bodies will tell us to keep going. We'll be stronger. We'll hum.

Chapter Twenty-Three
The Language of Us

The day I quit my job gave me far more peace than the day I showed up for it, that's for sure. But I felt guilty that I no longer had a paycheck and that the kids and I were going to have to scrimp. I also felt like I'd lost all ability to compete with my ex-husband for lifestyle—the kids were just going to have to realize that when they were with me, we weren't going to eat out or buy video games or go on trips.

But quitting my job gave me an opportunity that I was ready to take—the opportunity to write.

Touching the Trees

It wasn't lost on the people closest to me that writing was what I needed to do. In fact, Zane (who was very proud of me for landing the job, but who also understood why I had to quit) said to me, "Don't forget why you did all of this. Don't give up on your dreams."

He was right. I needed to take a risk and put my words to work for me—if for no other reason than to finally hear myself think.

I've always loved language. From the moment I could talk, I talked. From the moment I figured out what singing was, I stood at the end of the driveway and sang to the dandelion microphones drooping from my clenched hand. When I learned to read…it was heaven. I was that kid with the flashlight under the covers, who read the same book over and over again *(Little Girl Lost)* and couldn't believe that something I held in my hand could touch my little girl heart and imagination like that. On long car trips, I'd even hold my books up to the shine of the headlights behind us and get frustrated when the country roads were deserted.

That love affair with language grew when I learned how to formulate an original thought and write it down. My first play had something to do with mice, I remember. I think there might have even been installments. The best thrill of that first writing experience, though, was when my Uncle Dan read my mouse play to a roomful of relatives at a family reunion. I thought I was the greatest eight-year-old ever. Although I couldn't put it into words at that time (I was still writing about mice, after all), I saw that writing gave someone, like my eight-year-old self, the power to affect someone else.

Fast forward twenty years and that love affair with language became a bit of a love/hate relationship, particularly with writing. I worked in a public relations agency and hated it. I became an English teacher and loved it. I wanted to write fiction, non-fiction, poetry, and articles when my kids were little, but talked myself out of it. I wrote and thought my writing was fabulous when it was really crap. I took whole years off of writing for pleasure and then came up with a powerful seven line poem to underscore a desperate desire to fill my life with another child. And it worked.

Finally, four or five years ago, I got fed up with myself. My whining about "I want to be a writer! I want to be a writer!" was aggravating even me—mostly because I wasn't actually writing. So, while sitting at a bar, I decided to give up writing.

This was a big deal for me, which is why I can remember it so vividly. I broke up with writing because I was sick of that bastard ambition flitting around on the periphery of my boxed-up life as a wife and mother. I was tired of hearing its siren call and being frozen before even trying. I was done, clap-clap, with the dream.

Only I wasn't.

Within two months of that monumental decision, I realized I'd taken a wrong turn. So I enrolled in a writing class and haven't stopped writing since.

Touching the Trees

One outcome of forcing myself to write is that I find myself listening. Sometimes I listen because I'm just plain nosy. Sometimes I listen to try to capture how one of my characters might talk. Often I listen to hear if there's anything beneath the words being spoken.

One day, when I was out to lunch by myself, I listened to one woman try to explain to another that she felt judged at bible study. I heard her frustration and anguish when the other woman told her people weren't judging her, they just found her hard to talk to because she's so different from them. The first woman's response, which out loud was a lamenting "I know," sounded a lot like *"That's the judging I'm talking about!"* to me.

The languages we share fascinate me. For every two people, there's a different dialect, a different set of love words and anger words, humor words and trigger words. The language between a particular mother and a particular child is different from the language of the father to that same child. The language of my former mother-in-law sometimes drove me crazy, but it was still her language and I would recognize it to this day. (I think she deliberately mispronounced words for so long that she didn't actually remember how to say them correctly. My favorite was "swayve" instead of suave.)

When you're in a relationship with someone, anyone, you eventually develop a shared language that becomes your Language of Us.

I've got one with my kids, and it will evolve our whole lives. In fact, one of our key Us words is Bahooya. This poor, carnival-worker-sounding word is the outgrowth of an acronym my college sorority girlfriends and I created over 20 years ago. The original word was Pyhooya (it even looks slightly Greek, doesn't it?) and it stood for Pull Your Head Out Of Your Ass. I've used that word constantly for decades now. It's been used as a noun, "Don't be such a Bahooya!" nearly as often as it's been used as an exclamation—"Bahooya, you stupid driver!"

Now my daughter uses that word when she does something fantastic. Kind of like Emeril the Chef yelling, "Bam!", my girl yells "Bahooya!" when she sticks a round-off. My kids grew up saying it (not knowing what it meant until recently) and it's ours.

Language is the glue of our family relationship at times. I know when they get older, at least one of them will call to tell me some dumb trouble they've gotten into and my first reaction will be, "Why'd you have to go and be such a Bahooya?" Then, if it's not something horribly serious, they will know that everything's going to be okay (once they make restitution, of course...).

We've got other words too, but with each of my kids I have an even more specialized sub-dialect. My older son has longish, wavy hair that I have been inappropriately envious of since he was about six. Recently, I was watching YouTube and heard hair like his referred to as "lettuce." Forevermore, even if he gets a crew cut, he'll have lettuce to me.

My other son used to hate cows, so every time I see one I yell, "You no say MOO!" and he yells it back in his cracking teenager voice. Marco Polo, farm-style. I call my daughter "Boo" from the movie *Monsters, Inc.* because someone gave me a Boo shirt before I even knew she was a girl. Then she was one and the name fit.

It's our language and I love it.

My ex-husband and I had a language too. We had words cultivated over two decades of knowing each other. We had nicknames for old friends that only we ever spoke. We could say one word, the punch line to a joke, and know what the other was thinking. It was nice being able to speak shorthand to someone else.

As my marriage dissolved, I could hear particular patterns, certain surgically inserted words in our discussions, which were often my best clues as to how well a negotiation was going or if it was time to hang up the phone. Then our language lost its adhesiveness, and faltered altogether.

One of the oddest things I missed right after I left him, in addition to my hand-painted flower pots and a hedge-trimmer, was our shared language. It was too intimate, in the heat of arguments over 401k splits, to refer to our old codes. Quite often I felt word-lonely. Who would I laugh with over the mispronunciation of the capital of Columbia? Who could I shoot eyes at when his sister said "Nike" instead of "Nike-ee?" In the end, the death of our Us language signaled more to me than moving out or signing the papers. We were done and our language was lost.

Later, when I began my relationship with Peter, I remember realizing that some of the early awkward silences or difficulties choosing words in a conversation were because we didn't yet have a Language of Us. Within a couple of weeks of our first date, I told him that someday we would have our own language. Someday we would have our own words, our own shorthand, and our own way of communicating. I hope I told him I was looking forward to it, because I really wanted to achieve that level of intimacy. Our language, our Us language, would be special and telling. It would bring us closer and then be a barometer of how close we really were. And I knew that if we could achieve a strong Us language, our relationship would be a safe, good place to hang out.

Now that we've been together awhile, we do have our own Language of Us. He says he's hanging a light fixture, I know it means he's trying something new. If he asks where I'm going, I know he's not wondering if I'm headed out to the store—he wants to know if I've crawled into my head to think. When we talk about boxes, and we both know that I'm afraid of getting labeled and pigeonholed.

It's our language and I love it.

As long as we're in meaningful relationships, we'll build our shared language. We can listen carefully to one another other and learn to recognize when a particular phrase or word has the potential to enter our dictionary. Then, when the time comes to codify the word or phrase, we'll be able to place it there together, tenderly scrawled (or sometimes drunkenly, like in the case of the words "stickhead dickerhead"—Peter's and my new favorite party game) on a blank page inside an imaginary cover that says "Us."

And if no one turns out to be a Bahooya, we'll all have nice fat dictionaries in the end.

Chapter Twenty-Four
Sorry is an Easy Word to Hate

As much as I love to play with language, words also give me headaches. I don't like clichés and I don't like repetition. Certain speech patterns—like the long, slow way my ex-husband told stories, or the way some people finish my sentences like they're mind-readers, or how others finish their own sentences like questions—grate on my nerves after a very short while.

But I believe in the power of words and sentences to convey emotion and thoughts. I believe that whole discussions can turn on a phrase or an appropriate word choice.

Once I began writing again, written language became my friend in otherwise losing battles. I couldn't always be certain of winning a verbal argument, but if someone gave me a keyboard (and an email address) and I could usually hit the bulls-eye of what I want to say.

In the last few years, though, I've found that I'm philosophically opposed to certain uses of certain words, and they all have to do with apology. "My apologies, pardon me, please excuse my rudeness...." Every one of those has lost nearly all discernible relevance when they are used insincerely either by me or by others.

For all of the last twenty years, I've hated the word sorry most of all. I've hated it like the weak hate bullies. I've hated it like I hate solicitors calling at dinner time or knocking on my door. I've hated it like the first flip-flop blister of summer. Not deep-seated hate, obviously—which is the kind reserved for someone who's harmed my children or tortured a pet. But a niggling, annoying angst aimed at those things that seem impossible to eradicate from my life.

When I was married, I hated the word because it meant nothing. If I had to point out the wrong to elicit an apology, it sure didn't feel like he meant it if he then gave me one. "I'm sorry I...cheated, ignored you, overruled you, yelled at the kids when you had it under control, came home late without a call, drank too much, missed two baby showers, left you alone in the hospital, questioned your parenting, read your emails..."

On my way out of the marriage, I wrote down a list of every bad thing he'd ever done to me that I hadn't found it in myself to forgive. As we went through them, one by one on an afternoon while the kids were at school, he sometimes offered explanation and justification. More often, though, he just said he was sorry. I don't know exactly what I was looking for, but each sorry made me want to forgive him even less.

His sorry was, to him, the make-it-all-better card. It was his acknowledgement that he'd wronged me and realized it. It was supposed to staunch the blood flow of the current injury but it lacked any long-term healing powers. Sure, he probably felt bad for whatever it was that he was apologizing for—enough to say the words. But he was never sorry enough to change the behavior. So the words meant nothing.

Then I finally saw the pattern. He would do anything he could to get his way—whether it was argue with me, bulldoze the kids, strategize ways to make me acquiesce, or reduce me to a puddle of emotions too jumbled to make a decision. Then he would run me over. Much later, when I finally regained enough strength to call him on his lack of consideration, he would apologize. The end, so he thought. But it wasn't just the end of the situation—it was really the end to another bit of trust in him.

Now I'm in a different situation and I still hate the word sorry. Peter's an empath like myself. We anticipate other people's needs and try to make it all work so that everyone's happy. We're ultra-sensitive to feelings and body language and silence. But we've also said sorry like programmed automatons. We've used sorry as a shield. We haven't always apologized to ease the other person's pain—we've said it to pre-empt our own.

I don't like that either.

Peter and I have had a few experiences that dredged up painful memories of our old, separate married lives and caused us to revert back to weak. During those stretches, we were sometimes unable to connect as well as we wanted to because the logistics of being alone together didn't work out. So we got out of alignment and it caused us both to become fearful that something bad was happening to our relationship.

We said, "I'm sorry" a lot during those times. A lot. But we weren't, either of us, saying it because we'd done something wrong—because we hadn't. We were saying it so we could deflect the unknown. We were saying it because we were afraid that by being ourselves, we'd somehow become someone the other person didn't like so much anymore. We threw out apologies like candy to a parade crowd—here, take this token of my desire to preserve this relationship at all costs.

Those sorries, like the ones my ex-husband gave me, also didn't mean very much.

I know I felt bad, though. I felt bad that my moodiness wreaked havoc on his mood. I felt bad when I dwelled on the past and feared the future. I felt bad that things I said or did were triggers for his painful memories. I felt bad that, even after all the time we'd known each other, our footing sometimes felt so tenuous and slippery. I felt bad that I couldn't be strong all the time. I felt bad that he thought he needed permission to be strong for me.

I remember telling my ex-husband to stop saying sorry because it meant so little coming from someone so seemingly hell-bent on my destruction. Now *I* need to stop saying it because it means too much. It means that I'm unsure and afraid. It means that I don't trust everything will work out okay. It means that I still have some miles to walk before I'm where I want to be.

One day I offered to Peter a pact, a pinkie-swear, my hand instead of a brick wall. "Let's not say sorry right now," I told him. "Let's not apologize for our feelings because we'll end up further into this swirl of sorry-full gloom, giving up too much to keep the peace."

There's an old saying: "Love means never having to say you're sorry." I used to think it meant that a person should never cause his or her loved one any pain, ever. And I still do, if the pain is caused intentionally.

But I think this, too: Love means that we will never need or demand an apology from someone we love for how he or she feels. Love means never wanting someone in the position of having to apologize for how we feel, either. For Peter and me, love means reserving the word "sorry" for when I accidentally pinch his arm while it's around me or he runs out of time to help me put in a dimmer switch.

    Love means setting ourselves free from the need to apologize for being just who we are.

Chapter Twenty-Five
The Ease of Ordinary Things

There's a beauty in the ease of ordinary things. There is fluidity of purpose, muscles flexing and reacting in time-tried patterns to create natural movement. You can see someone's inner beauty when he or she is going about the ordinary life. It's where people are most comfortable, where they don't have to think about doing, where they just do.

It's that place where it doesn't matter who we think we are, because we just *are*.

Touching the Trees

You can catch just about anyone in that place if you watch long enough. It's in morning routines— shaving, applying lotion/makeup/aftershave, pulling on pants, buttoning shirts, and inserting earrings. It's in meals—chewing slowly, blowing on hot coffee, licking foam off upper lips, or picking up four fries at a time, every time. It's in hobbies—planting gardens, running, painting, and reading novels. Beauty comes when the action is so practiced, so ordinary, as to be indistinguishable from breathing or sleeping or being at peace.

Relationships can have that same ease, that same beauty, in the ordinary. I've seen it with Peter and my children each time they transition into a deeper realm—into a friendship that is safe in its easiness. Sometimes they do nothing but talk about video games, compare new electronics, or hang out in the backyard, but the sheer nothingness of that time together—without anxiety, defensiveness, protectiveness, or posturing—is beautiful to behold.

I've seen that same ease build between Peter and me, too. Even a few months into our relationship, I was self-conscious about nearly everything. Although we were friends long before we were anything else, so much of what Peter and I did together was new. We weren't sure if the other would like movie-theater popcorn drenched in butter and crunchy with salt—turns out we both do. We weren't comfortable making dinner— once I caused a grease fire (the first one of my life) because I was so nervous. We weren't at ease late at night when we fell asleep on the couch and worried that the other one heard us snore. We checked, double-checked, and triple-checked to make sure everything was okay. And it was.

Little by little, encounter after encounter, we built trust and the ease of our ordinary times together grew into something natural. The most remarkable thing is that we've both seen reflections on the faces of those who catch us in those seconds of honest being—the smiles, the nods, the sly grins—that tell us that it's visible. It's the ease of the ordinary and it's beautiful.

There were plenty of ordinary things in my marriage. But there was so much tension and control and frustration that the routine of how we lived together resembled more tigers pacing a cage than two otters swimming lazy circles around each other, coming close with great frequency to snuggle and wrestle and enjoy. The unease wasn't pretty. It was draining and sickness-inducing and mind-numbing in its potential perpetuity. We harbored our disconnection in hooded eyes, forays away from the relationship, and systems of surveillance and espionage.

I can see the difference between my life now and my life then. I can see that habit and routine don't always have to mean being stuck. Rather, they can ring in the transition from self-conscious to unconscious—from frown lines to gracefulness. They might just be the threshold between worry and trust.

Being in the habit of trusting someone who's trustworthy? Or of loving someone who loves you back? What about being in the routine of giving without expectation? That's a beautiful way to live.

Of course, we will still sometimes feel out-of-place—especially as we try new things in our new lives. I sensed the hitch in my step when I walked into my first "biker" bar. I could tell that my hips didn't have their regular sway; my shoulders were too tight and my steps too stilted. Sometimes I wasn't sure what to say and tended to order my beer wrong...was it Grain Belt Premium or Premium Grain Belt? When none of it felt ordinary, none of it was easy.

But I can finally see the beauty in what *is* easy and what *is* ordinary—slipping my hand into Peter's, jumping up and cheering when my kids do something particularly well, or even brushing my daughter's sweaty bangs off her forehead when she sleeps.

We can relish the chance to make happiness, love and trust into our ordinary things—for them to become as second-nature as brushing our teeth or swallowing a sip of coffee or soda. We can watch for the beauty that will unfold as those new ordinaries create for us an easy, natural state of being. Because that beauty will be there. It will mean we're on our way.

Part IV.
Standing Up

Chapter Twenty-Six
Walls and Bridges
(And a Couple of Fences, Too)

There's still work that has to be done before settling into an easy, beautiful new chapter in my life. One of my constant struggles is with staying "open." When I feel stressed out, cornered or afraid, it's my nature to close my borders. I retreat into my head, sometimes to the point where I even retreat from being touched or comforted. I don't know that it's always a bad thing to take time to identify my feelings and make decisions about what to do.

But it takes a conscious effort to come back—to crank open the gates and let people in.

A few years ago during a therapy session, Zane suggested I read *Boundaries in Marriage*, by Henry Gould and Peter Townsend. The books' premise was that people need to have a fence around their most protected areas—whether it's their emotions, their social lives, their faith, their fears, their families, or their decisions. Inside those fenced borders lie portions of the self that are not under anyone else's control. For instance, I can see my neighbors' yards with the play sets, fire pits, and occasional dandelions, because fences are see-through. Those neighbors can see my long grass and rope swing because my fence is see-through, too. But my yard is under my control and those yards are under somebody else's.

Trust plays a big part in respecting someone else's boundaries. If I trust that people are capable of taking care of their own yards, then I won't scramble up and over the fence to mow it for them or get overly concerned when the leaves haven't been picked up late into fall. But if we don't trust each other, we might as well just build ourselves a wall.

If you live in Minneapolis, you know that there's been a massive highway construction project going on at the intersection of two major downtown interstates.

One component of the highway project is the building of massive walls to protect residents of the quiet neighborhoods adjacent to the highway from the additional noise that an enlarged road system creates. The walls' roles are to separate the daily life of walking the kids to school, hanging laundry from the line, and sitting on the porch having a beer, from interference caused by rumbling hordes of commuters.

The walls, like fences, provide separation, too. Walls are just a different kind of boundary. By design, walls are impenetrable. Those walls on I35W are several stories tall and made out of hundreds of thousands of interlocking blocks, steel reinforcements, and wooden buttresses. They are solid except for the weep-holes that are designed to keep them from buckling.

The walls that ended my marriage were just as impenetrable. My ex-husband used control, anger, and money to keep me from getting too close to his core. He was a world-class negotiator at work—plotting out multi-million dollar deals like a well-played poker game. A lot of bluff, a lot of bluster, but always the same: an array of cards that he could convince anyone was a winning hand. While we were married, if he disagreed with a decision I made or the methodology I used to make it, he argued or sulked or did things his way anyway and managed to convince me I was wrong. Each time he did, another block or more got added to the wall between us.

Every few years or so I'd have enough of that ongoing construction and march us into couples therapy. Those times were our weep-holes. They were a chance to see behind the walls, even if it was just a wet eyeball pressed against where some mortar was missing. But we were never able to tear the whole thing down. I couldn't, or wouldn't, get rid of the blocks that kept me from seeing that he cheated on me because he must not have loved me. He wouldn't, or couldn't, get rid of the blocks that kept him from seeing that I was wasting away emotionally and intellectually while I waited for him to slow down, take a breath, and notice me. He was going north at breakneck speed and I was going south on the frontage road hoping the construction guys would whistle. The wall kept us from seeing each other and colliding. We weren't happy, but we were safe from having to be emotionally vulnerable.

Whether or not you live in Minnesota, you probably remember the I35W bridge collapse on August 1, 2007. That bridge collapse killed 13 people and injured 145 others. Coincidentally, construction on the new bridge started at about the same time as I was looking for ways out of the marriage. It hasn't been lost on me that a bridge of any magnitude is better to have between people who care about each other than a wall.

I've noticed when I've needed to bridge a gap in understanding with someone or when I've needed help (that I resist asking for) is that every opportunity to build a wall is also an opportunity to build a bridge. It's just that the outcomes are different.

With my children, I have those opportunities every day. Do I shut down when they tell me about their dad's girlfriend or do I find ways to help them feel okay about that relationship? Do I hide from their questions about my own relationship with Peter or do I answer honestly? One day, after Peter and I had been together for many months, my middle child asked me if I was on birth control pills (by the way—what kind of question is *that* to ask your mom?). That led into a discussion about when I had my tubes tied, ended up with an ectopic pregnancy, and underwent emergency life-saving surgery, all things he didn't know. It was a bridge between the two of us. He was reaching out to talk about sexuality. I listened and shared.

Unfortunately, I could never have had that discussion with my own mother when I was a teenager because she'd already built the wall of, "The only safe birth control is an aspirin held tightly between your knees." I never made it past that wall to talk with her openly about love and sex.

Speaking of my mom, I put up a giant wall with her several years ago. I shut her out because I couldn't take her judgment and her manipulation (the experts call it triangulation) of me and my siblings. She hadn't been supportive or protective for as long as I could remember and I had no use for what I perceived as conditional love.

That wall was firmly in place when I told her I was getting divorced, so I decided that I didn't want to tell her any of the details about the collapse of my marriage. Then she did what she did best—started with the matter-of-fact questioning and proceeded to guilt-inducing martyrdom. "Maybe you don't need to talk about it, but I do. I need to know why this is happening." It seemed to be all about her. I didn't believe that she wanted to know so she could comfort me. I believed that she wanted to know so she could judge me.

However, it turns out my silence was all about me too—my need to wall myself off from her and protect my children and myself from whatever judgment she was going to apply to the truth.

Then one day I just stopped. I quit slathering grout onto our cracked relationship and told her everything. I told her about the early infidelities. I explained that I never wanted to have a marriage like hers and ended up having one anyway. I laid out my dreams and my hopes for a future free of the kind of control I'd been living under.

Her response? "I wish I had your courage. I wish I could have done that for myself a long time ago." My mom and I built a bridge. We did it by taking down a wall.

Peter and I made a pact, even before our first date, that if we decided to go ahead with a relationship, we were going to build it deliberately and with honesty. Peter had two prior relationships with exceedingly controlling women from whom he'd learned to hide emotionally. I had twenty years of a controlling situation myself.

So at the beginning of our own relationship, we were like two Whack-a-moles at the carnival. We'd poke our heads up, share a little bit of ourselves, and retreat back into the hole to see if we'd get hit. We never got hit, though, because neither of us ever even picked up the mallet. And each time that we trusted we were being accepted, we sunk footers for a bridge between us. Eventually we began heaving ropes across the river to each other from our fenced-off psyches. Here, take this one and tie it off. Here's a support beam. Here's a plank. Test the weight. Here's my hand. Here's my beating heart.

It hasn't always been easy, though, because we have much more experience building walls. Over time he has asked about different aspects of my marriage. I haven't always told him the whole truth right away (wall). But I've gone back to fill in the blanks and, much more importantly, to explain to him why I was scared to tell him the first time around (bridge).

Eventually he came over for his first dinner with me and my kids. It went okay, except that my anxiety grew to the point where I hid it from him for two days while I thought about why I was feeling that way (wall). He finally decided that we needed to clear the air, so we talked about it—the assumptions I was making about his feelings, which box I was putting myself into, and where we could go from there (bridge).

He has made decisions about his schedule —work, social, or both—and done the quadruple check with me afterwards. "Are you sure it's okay that I went? Are you positive? I could have done this instead…Next time I could…" He does this to make sure I'm not like his ex-wife and that he doesn't need to haul a block over and place it squarely between us just to be able to function on his own. He does that checking in to test me and my reactions (wall). Unlike her, I trust that he knows how to take care of himself and his life (bridge). And each bit of trust is a spider thread that makes us stronger.

I challenged myself to work on building emotional bridges as I moved through the transition to a new, richer life. I wasn't always successful, but I think recognizing that I had a choice to wall off or connect was half the battle. When we feel like we have to protect our inner core from being hurt, a wall seems like the only option. But to move forward, to grow, we need to be willing to build bridges and connections to people who care about us.

We can't forget, though, to keep healthy boundaries around those things in our lives that are most important. After all, fences are okay, too.

Touching the Trees

Chapter Twenty-Seven
Superfamily

Many years ago, when I started dating my ex-husband, his family was in the habit of having "family dinner" every Friday night. I wasn't invited, even though they'd known me for years. It wasn't until we were engaged that I was welcome to share a meal with them. Even then, if it was a holiday dinner, I was asked to take the pictures of the family but wasn't included in the photos. I wasn't really "family" until we were married—when I began legally using their last name. I have to say, though, that even the act of getting married by a priest in a quasi-Catholic ceremony didn't solidify my

Touching the Trees

place. I memorized the pre-meal prayer but was the only one who didn't cross herself. I was family, but not *family* family.

I've struggled for years and years with where my kids and I fit into that family. Sometimes we were excluded simply because we didn't live near them. Easter egg hunts with plastic eggs filled with money, gift certificates, and candy provided the local grandchildren with a great experience. My children, at their grandparents' next visit, received a plastic bag with odds and ends of treats—a few Lindt truffles, a 6-pack of Oreos, a Snickers, and a bag of M&Ms. Sometimes that didn't even happen until May or June. Nearby nieces, nephews, and daughters-in-law were taken out to lunch or to a museum—time with my kids was squeezed in-between their grandparents' other travel plans.

Recently I ran into some people I know at a bar after a lacrosse game—a woman named Heide, her dad Barry, and a couple of young guys I'd never seen before. At one point in the casual conversation, one of the guys a little drunkenly pointed at Barry and said, "Superfamily!" Barry pointed right back at him and said, "Superfamily!"

I raised my eyebrows at Heide and she just laughed. "My dad's created a Superfamily, but I'm not in it. Just my sister, him, and apparently this guy." She jerked her thumb to the guy on her right.

I never got a coherent definition of Superfamily from Barry that night at the bar, but it got me thinking.

In almost all cases, people are classified as family if they are blood relatives or if they are legally recognized as family. Now that I'm divorced, though, I believe there are other ways to define family—which is why I'm intrigued by the concept of a Superfamily. What if you could create your own family? What if you can belong together even without any blood, legal, or religious ties?

One Easter after my divorce, the idea of what makes a family became a question for me again. My children were with their father and his girlfriend for the holiday. Peter had his son for the day and wanted very much to invite me over, but his son wanted the day to be "just family." So I went to a movie. On the way there I passed groups of people eating at long tables on driveways, kids running around chasing other kids, couples and older children walking down the street and, in one picturesque scene, a teenager sitting on his front stoop playing guitar for a little boy who twirled a leafless branch while he listened. I felt terribly alone and very family-less.

On Easter night, after Peter took his son back to his ex-wife's house, I asked him, "When will we be considered enough of a family for him to be okay with me being part of days like today?" Neither of us knew the answer.

Over twenty years ago I had the same question: If you aren't related by blood or law, is there a point in time when you can become family anyway? Or are you stuck being out until society decides you can be in?

One thing about being in a family, though, is that you don't have an easy escape route. There is a level of commitment that comes with being in a family. I couldn't sever my legal relationship with my ex-husband without the tribulations of a divorce. I couldn't turn my back on my parents, regardless of how angry I might be at them at times, without still feeling obligated to donate a kidney if necessary. There's a saying that you can choose your friends but you can't choose your family. (I've also heard that you can pick your friends and you can pick your nose, but you can't pick your friend's nose…) But I've noticed that I'm picking and being picked by people who aren't technically family—or who aren't technically family anymore. I feel a commitment to them and from them that I want to honor, too.

Without question, Peter would be at the top of my list if I were to build my Superfamily. We're not married, nor can I say the words "boyfriend" or "girlfriend" without having a little arrhythmia. He's just him and I'm just me, but we are building a relationship that seems to transcend friendship and companionship.

One of the first times we spent a few hours alone together I gave him a long hug, inhaled behind his ear, and felt like I'd come home. His generosity, kindness, and senses of inclusiveness and adventure felt like family to me even when we were "just friends."

Touching the Trees

Although there are still times his son hasn't quite accepted me and a different paradigm of what a family can be, I think that will happen if, as Peter says, we just show him that it's possible, healthy, and good.

My friend Sasha would absolutely be in my Superfamily. I trust her completely and I want to give back to her every emotional and physical support she's ever given me—and there have been plenty of both. If I had to pick one girlfriend whose old-lady self I'd want to be old-lady best friends with, it would be her. (When I told her I was writing about what "family" meant, she said, "Jesus, it means whatever you want it to!") She gets it.

My friends, Ron and Amanda, are definitely in my Superfamily. They have picked up the pieces for me a hundred or more times since the separation and divorce. Their children are like my own and vice versa. If there's an emergency, I can call them and they will help, no questions asked. We're the kind of Superfamily where the kids can sleep over with no prior arrangement, toothbrush, or clean underwear. They can even stay for three days if necessary. Other cultures and Hillary Clinton call us a village. Ron calls us his second family. I call my kids by their kids' names by accident.

Kat (an unwavering friend for over 30 years), Camille, James and Tiana, Kurt and Trisha, Adam, much of Peter's family... If I think about it long enough, I've got a really nice extended Superfamily.

Believe it or not, my former mother-in-law is also in my Superfamily. Since the divorce she's continued to reach out to me. Fairly regularly, I get a note from her asking how my life is going and telling me about hers. Sometimes I get a holiday card or a little gift. When I was still married to her son, it was easy to undervalue the emails and cards because they seemed so superficial—she always asked questions about the weather, work, or the kids. Now I see those connections differently. Now I value them as signs that she's expanding her previous definition of family. She's letting me out of the non-Catholic daughter-in-law box she put me in when I married her oldest child.

Twenty-four years ago I wasn't welcome at her dining room table. But a few months ago she visited me at my new house, we had some coffee, and I showed her the white bleeding-heart plant I'd just discovered in my backyard.

I have some wonderful "real" family—siblings, children, cousins, aunts, uncles, and still one rather feisty grandmother.

But I also have people in my life that I know would lay down theirs for mine, who can accept me without reservation, and for whom I would do the same at any moment. They're my other family. My Superfamily.

I couldn't do this without them.

Chapter Twenty-Eight
The Last Jalapeno

One of my favorite childhood memories was going to my great-grandparents' annual Christmas party. It was always held in November so all the families could celebrate Christmas at home. It was also always held at a golf course, which gave us kids plenty of room to run around (once all the food was eaten) so the adults could settle into grownup talk.

In retrospect, what was amazing about those parties was that my great-grandparents managed to find something personal for each of us great-grandchildren, even as our numbers swelled into the dozens.

Touching the Trees

My favorite gift was the one I got at the last party before my great-grandfather passed away. It was a simple houseplant in a decorative plastic gallon pot with gold trim and it ignited in me a desire to garden that continues to this day.

When I bought my house, I liked that it had enough bedrooms for everyone to have his or her own and plenty of bathroom space for all of us to use. I also liked that its previous owners were master gardeners and much of the yard was landscaped beautifully and thoughtfully.

But one thing I'd always wanted to have at my home was a flourishing, bountiful vegetable garden. So as soon as my first spring thaw there finally happened, I rented myself a heavy tiller and went to work creating my dream garden. It took two days of arm-tingling, back-aching, hamstring-pulling work, but I got it done. In typical over-zealous gardening fashion, I planted way too much…five types of tomatoes, corn, pumpkins, cucumbers, lettuce, Brussels sprouts, carrots, cauliflower, green beans, two types of chives, basil, strawberries, raspberries, and one jalapeno plant.

I'll eat everything in that whole garden except the jalapenos, which begs the question of why I planted them in the first place. The answer is that I planted the three-inch starter plant because two of my kids love them and, frankly, it's a fun plant to grow. It's hardy and prolific, and gives relatively quick gratification to the gardener. (I needed quick gratification after some critter destroyed all of my corn stalks and ate most of my carrot tops a month into the growing season....) In the middle of summer, in the middle of the garden, while everything else is just budding out and starting the incline toward succulence and healthfulness, the only plant that's producing rapidly and is ready to harvest is the jalapeno.

So in July I picked the biggest, most ripe jalapeno, placed it carefully in a plastic baggie and gave it to...my ex-husband.

To be honest, I didn't think much of it at first. I only ever grew jalapenos (formerly in pots) for the people in my life who liked them. Those people were always my sons and their dad. (The one time I used them to make homemade salsa, my hands burned for days because of the juices and seeds. I gorged on salsa that year, but rarely ate jalapenos after that.) My habit was always to pick them, give them to the boys and their dad, and let them figure out how to eat them without suffering blisters and life-changing esophageal Scoville burns.

The night I picked that first jalapeno of the season, my boys weren't going to be with me, so I sent it with them to their dad's house so they could enjoy it there. It seemed like a reasonable thing to do at the time.

But here's the thing I don't understand. That jalapeno was the very first thing I harvested out of my very first self-made garden. It was more than a vegetable; it was a symbol of my independence and my personal and emotional growth. And I gave it away to the one person in this world that sometimes I cannot stand at even the most basic level.

What was I thinking?

Part of me wonders if it really was just the habit, like always. As in, here's something I don't like that they do like so I should give it to them, even if "them" includes him. Part of me wonders if I sent it as a subtle message—that I grew this thing without any help from him and, in fact, did it despite his best efforts to thwart my happiness in this life without him.

But part of me also wonders if I still want to believe there's something trustworthy and deserving in him. It's a little confusing to think that my first instinct remains mired in the hope that he's not as bad as he's shown himself to be, consistently, for so long.

After I left my ex-husband to begin this independent life, we had an encounter at a pool party at his house. I was there simply to pick up the kids, who attended the party. He was angry with me for a lot of things, not the least of which was that I'd gone and left him for good. At his invitation, and to calm my nerves, I had a couple of beers. Then it all went downhill. The kids fell asleep, the rest of the guests left, we fought, and I sobbed. Then I drank some more, we went swimming, we talked about the past and all of our good memories, and…well…just…and. It was quite possibly the most shameful night of my life.

See, I was already in a very young relationship with Peter. I'd let him in and encouraged him to let me in too. Our friendship had begun to evolve into something so special that we could barely find words to describe it. I was learning how to trust and he was learning how to open up. We were fragile separately and even more fragile as a unit.

Even as I entered the abyss of that pool after-pity-party, I wondered aloud who I was cheating on…the man who was technically still my husband or the man I wanted to be with. How had I managed to still feel like a cheater after trying so hard not to?

My ex-husband knew about my relationship with Peter. He knew that I was seeing someone he used to consider his friend. There have been times when I've believed that he wanted to ruin any chance of happiness I had with Peter by tainting me that night—by causing me to wonder if I was the exact same type of person I'd come to loathe.

Two days later, when we spoke about that night, he asked me if I'd "confessed" to Peter yet. He told me that he'd shared information about our encounter with his girlfriend and strongly encouraged me to do the same. I remember looking at him and wondering if he really thought it was okay to test his girlfriend that way. Then I realized that even worse than testing his own girlfriend, he was forcing me into either lying to Peter about that night or telling the truth—nearly guaranteeing that I would lose the one person in my life who had been unconditionally supportive up to that point.

He hated me that much. Yet, I gave him my first jalapeno.

A few months after that encounter, he accused me of putting my volunteer activities in front of my children. He threatened that I would have to cancel an out-of-town meeting or not see my kids for three weekends in a row. I begged him to stop taking such a hard line. I pleaded with him using logic. Then I pleaded with him by saying that my kids didn't need to be punished for his anger at me. He gave me back only one night with the kids.

Yet, I gave him my first jalapeno.

Most recently, he has taken to "giving" my daughter to his girlfriend at functions where we are both in attendance. If it's his custodial time with the kids, his girlfriend gets to control what my daughter does and eats, and who she talks to and sits with. Sometimes it's not me she picks, even though I'm within feet of her. It's beyond heart-breaking to be ignored or unchosen by my own child, in favor of her dad's girlfriend.

Yet, he got my first jalapeno.

Each encounter I have with my ex is a reason to sweat and work on calming my heart from its fight-or-flight response. He has accused me of being an uncaring mother, a free-loader, disrespectful, offensive, and inconsiderate. There are very few discussions between us that aren't layered with his simmering accusations that I treat him like a pariah or that I am depriving my children of something essential for their happiness.

So it's about time I stop believing in his innate trustworthiness and deservedness until he actually proves to me that he's capable of them. It may just be time to give up the last tendril of hope that he understands (or cares to understand) how I think and feel. I need to remember that he has chosen to corner, manipulate, and disparage me to get what he wants. I need to remind myself that he hates me because I dared to do the un-thinkable—leave him in order to find happiness on my own.

And I need, more than anything else, for that first jalapeno to be the last jalapeno.

Touching the Trees

Chapter Twenty-Nine
Hay Pillows and Splat Corners

    When I started on this journey, I focused on changing all the things I didn't like about myself and my life. Once many of those changes were made, though, it was time for the next step. It was time to plan for the future. I needed to visualize what I wanted my life to look like then I needed to make a plan to get there.

    The world of imagined possibilities opened up once when I got divorced, again when I left my job, and several times after that when I climbed onto the back of Peter's motorcycle and dove deeply into my needs, wants, desires, hopes, and fears.

Touching the Trees

I found out later that riding on the back of a motorcycle can induce a trance-like state not unlike hypnosis. For me, it allowed the exploration of the routes and paths of my journey—where I wanted to continue to move forward and where I needed to step back and choose another trail. Almost with fail, those times of uninterrupted thought (I couldn't very well bring the laptop and write, although I wanted to, very badly) brought clarification to a problem or a new perspective on an old feeling.

It also showed me that I didn't want to replace my old life completely.

I'm a big fan of the destination vacation. I love picking out a place to go, preferably warm in the winter or just plain "cool", and making whatever arrangements necessary to get there. Flight, car ride, or a combination of both—it doesn't matter. I'm happy to endure the travel headaches, if they come, just to be able to arrive where I want to be, change into whatever I want to wear there, and flop myself onto a chaise lounge, hopefully close to water, with a cold drink in my hand.

In the last few years, though, I've become a convert to the journey vacation. I realize I might be rather late to that party—understanding that the path is often just as important as the destination—but I finally arrived, ready to watch out the window or through a visor and enjoy the view.

Not only do I appreciate the journey vacation, but I've even figured out my two favorites so far. They are: a motorcycle drive through river country and a car drive through the Black Hills of South Dakota.

On the motorcycle, I love the canopied winding roads that dance, very gently, with the river bank. Sometimes the rustic roads lead away from the water, up into the hills, around farm after farm. But they always come back down, angling at various grades of steep until you're deposited within sight and smell of the water again. Often there's a railroad track separating you from the river, but that's even better. Nothing says Americana more to me than a front yard with a train running through it and a backyard that the river shares with you when it's not knocking on your door in early spring.

In the car, I love the steep inclines and the possibility of sneaking up on a slow-moving bison party in the Black Hills. Meandering through Custer State Park, trying to find The Herd, I've been known to settle for some wild donkeys that act like sidewalk t-shirt peddlers in New York City. "Look at me, madam! I've got what you need!" Those donkeys walk right up to your car windows if you dare make eye contact. "I'm wildlife! I'm best friends/cousins/in-laws with the bison you seek! I can get you 'in' if you just open your window a crack and share with me some of that puffcorn your lovely daughter is munching in the back seat."

I've appreciated the wild hares, turkeys, deer, goats, and rodents. But nothing compares to coming around a curve, seeing brake lights and realizing that a piece of history—a throwback to the old West—is standing in the middle of the road, sizing up your minivan like so much riff-raff, and deciding to keep right on keepin' on at whatever pace he darn well pleases.

I love everything about those journeys. Well, maybe except the fighting in the backseat if the kids are along. Maybe also the motion sickness if the driving is necessarily erratic due to conditions beyond our control. Okay, and maybe these two things:

Hay pillows and splat corners.

See, when I'm out in the country or up in the hills or down by the river, a part of my brain takes over that says, "Wouldn't it be great to live here?" It all looks so peaceful, so relaxed, so earthy, and so authentic. There's such a draw to a lifestyle that doesn't include four seasons of youth sports, music lessons, church classes, volunteering everywhere, an ex-husband within spitting distance, and running, running, running. On the journey, I can picture myself tending garden all day, taking a break for some lemonade or a cold beer mid-afternoon, cooking up a supper that includes more colors than freezer tan, and enjoying my family life to the fullest. There's a part of me that promises, on those trips, that I would never tire of bison leaving steaming presents in my yard or train conductors leaning on the air horn or wild hares digging holes in my garden, if I could just live there for a little while.

Touching the Trees

I've been accused several times of being someone who thinks the grass is greener somewhere else. I *have* thought that—that there's something better out there for me, whether it's a better understanding of myself, a better relationship with my kids, or a better sense of ownership over my circumstances or life—and I'm not ashamed of it. If I didn't think the grass was greener on the other side of transition, where would my motivation be to grow and change?

Anyway, when I get into fantasy-land and think that I could just up and move away from suburbia and enjoy the quiet life, those two things—the hay pillow and the splat corner—bring me right back to reality.

The hay pillow, if you're unfamiliar with it like I was, is this big white capsule of stuff (presumably hay, although I think the technical term is silage) that livestock farmers have instead of bales. They look like Paul Bunyan's sausages stuffed in white poly wrapping. When farmers need to dig out whatever's in there, they open one end and begin removing the contents of the hay pillow to feed the cows, horses, goats, llamas, etc. The hay pillow reminds me that there's no such thing as the quiet life tending your tomato plants when you're on the farm. There are animals to feed *every day*, crops to manage, and chores out the ying-yang. The hay pillow is something you have to open and use until it's gone. Then you have to get another hay pillow and start all over again—forever or as long as you run that homestead. There's nothing glamorous to me about the hay pillow.

But if I'm tempted to leave the middle-America river farmer life behind and head to the hills, here's the other problem. More commonly known as switchbacks or S-curves, I think of those roads that wind themselves up one side and down another through the hills and mountains as splat corners.

Why? Because you could get splatted at a moment's notice, of course. Most of those curves are blind and most of the outside edges of the roads are sheer drops into forest oblivion. Faced with oncoming traffic that might have drifted a smidge into your lane, your choices are splat with the semi, pickup, SUV, or station wagon…or splat into the woods, rolling over and over until you come to a complete stop simply because your vehicle has been impaled by a thirty-foot tall fir tree.

As much as I love the Black Hills, there's no way I could live with the constant worry that I'm going to get splatted. Or worse, that my kids or other loved ones are.

Those journey vacations are incredible, but they aren't leading me to greener grass in Wisconsin or Iowa or Illinois or Minnesota. They aren't leading me to go all Wild West and move to Wyoming or South Dakota to rustle herds of something through the passes. They just serve to remind me that it's okay to seek something better, as long as you have a little idea of what it is that you're looking for. I don't need a better farm because I don't have a farm now. I don't need a better overlook because I don't have an overlook now. I don't need a better pet bison because…well, you know.

One day, after having just survived an S-curve with an impressive, puckering, fear factor, I realized this: The greener grass I'm looking for comes from fertilizing, pruning, re-seeding, watering, and rest. It's certainly not a destination vacation. It's maybe not even a journey vacation. It's a transition, though, to the other side.

The other side doesn't have to be a completely new life with a completely new identity. We can make the lives we have the best they can be, simply by recognizing what is good, what is worth keeping, and what can be improved. Then we can love and enjoy them and really *live* in them.

Touching the Trees

Chapter Thirty
Tubing the Wake

    I don't want to minimize the benefits of thinking time on destination vacations, though. Beyond people-watching, vacation is a great opportunity to hide behind closed eyelids and contemplate.

    One summer I was able to join Peter on his family vacation in California. Since my kids weren't with me, I was able to sit by the lake, read a book, and think about nothing and everything.

    Then I got antsy.

    And my elbows are still scarred.

On my last day there, I went tubing on the giant lake behind a powerful, roaring wakeboarding boat. Sharing a tube with me was Peter's niece, who'd asked me to tube with her. "It's girl-power time!" she said.

The first tube we rode was called the Atom. It was blue and triangular and each point had an inflated ball. It looked a lot like a jack from the jacks game and was an easy ride. The second tube we rode, called the Extreme, was a little trickier since it didn't have any inflated balls to keep us in place.

Each tube (basically a rubber inflatable with a slickly designed cover) had nylon handles for holding on. My compadre and I each picked out two handles to start with, but eventually crossed over our arms to use the other person's handles so we could keep our bodies more centered on the tubes during the rides.

Most tubers will agree that one of the best things about tubing is the turns. Sure, it's fun to go Mach-5 across an empty, glass-like expanse of lake, but all that gets the rider is dry bangs and sunburns on the backs of his or her legs. Our boat captain knew this (being a seasoned tube- and wakeboard-puller), so he took us back and forth in lazy figure eights, cutting across our own wakes and letting us get as much air as we could handle.

We definitely got some air. One time we flew so high after hitting a big wave that when we landed I was fairly certain my back was broken. It wasn't, obviously (and thank goodness). But I did utter the "S" word more than once in the company of my young riding partner—followed quickly by that other "S" word (which, in this case, was appropriate). "Sorry!"

However, in addition to big air we also got some screeching, tight turns that weren't so lazy and that threatened to fly us off the tube and into the lake.

Any time there's a turn, no matter how slow it might seem to the boat, there's a chance of the tube going outside the wake, picking up enormous amounts of force, and becoming impossible to hold onto. So our goal was to ride the wake and not fall off the other side of it. Think of it as banking on a race-track, only if we went too far there was no wall to crash into—we just went into the lake on our backs, turtle-style.

A couple of times that very thing happened—we got outside the wake going too fast and my companion went into the drink. Since the boat was filled with a bunch of teenage and pre-teenage boys, though, I felt unreasonably compelled to show how tough I was for a mom. So I held on for absolute dear life, nearly broken back, spasm-ing bladder, and all.

After all that tubing, my elbows were killing me from coming into constant, wet contact with rough nylon for 5-10 grueling minutes. It was like when I played basketball in middle school—I constantly had skinned knees from sliding on the wood floor trying to wrestle rebounds away from opponents. It's the same thing in tubing; just that a different body part becomes skinned. It's no less painful, though.

Touching the Trees

For several weeks after that vacation, I could feel the raw spots on my elbows where the skin hadn't quite finished growing back yet. Every twinge reminded me of screeching with laughter and blinking away needles of lake spray. Those twinges also reminded me of the fear of going outside the wake.

In my not-on-vacation real life, I've tubed the wake a little bit when I considered a few big decisions, like blending my life with Peter's. I've been excited about the possibility of waking up with him nearly every morning and curling in next to him nearly every night. I've been happy about the prospect of getting to do a relationship "right" this time—in a way that works for both people in the couple and that also provides good role models for our children. I've been hopeful that at least half of our kids will be extremely accepting of our future relationship and that the other half will come to like it (or at least not hate it).

See, when I was on that vacation, I had an epiphany. I finally *really* believed that I was in charge of my own destiny. I finally *really* believed that I was able to make decisions about my future and my children's futures using my own sound logic and intuition. I finally *really* believed that I owned my life. And I pulled those beliefs tight and made a commitment to myself and to Peter that I wanted to share my life, my hard-won and joyous life, with him.

But after that epiphany came the tiniest bit of my old anxieties. I began to worry that I might fall off the tube and drown in a fear of losing myself.

The reality is that I get afraid of taking on more than I can handle. I get afraid that, despite our deep affection for each other and our pinky-swears to always talk things through, we'll butt up against something that we can't overcome, like a troublesome ex, unsteady finances, or a lost focus. I'm even a bit nervous about learning a new daily routine, having done that several times in the last few years. I worry about trying to make sure I don't sabotage my professional goals by focusing so much on my personal choices. And I'm struggling with how soon the kids can add more changes to their lives.

I keep reminding myself, though, like a parent encouraging her child to try something a little scary and new, that the chances of losing myself in a life that I consciously chose really are quite low.

One of the best things a tuber can do to keep from falling off the tube at the apex of the turn is to stick his or her inside foot into the water to provide some stability and drag. The further into the water one's foot and leg goes, the higher the chances that the tube will stay upright.

So I've stuck my foot in the water swirling around these life decisions I'm making about and with Peter. Call it being grounded or call it being realistic, but I've generally been able to come out of my imaginary

Middle Age Faux-Bride magazine (with its ideas for dresses, non-traditional vows, and family-building activities) to remember the hard work that needs to be done—physically to the house and emotionally with the kids and ourselves—to be able to make our future together a reality.

To control our fear of change, we need to remember that as much as we're on the tube, we're also driving the boat. Those figure eights, cutting across wakes, are under our control too. That's essential for us to know. If we push too far too fast, we have no one to blame but ourselves. But we also have the power to cut the engine and reel ourselves back in to where it's safe and manageable—for any reason and at any time.

I'm hopeful that the process of changing my life for the better is more like riding the Atom than the Extreme. I'd like to think that I have some inflated bumpers, namely a commitment to open and honest communication with myself and others, to keep me from tipping over and getting lost in whitecaps.

There can be a sense of peace knowing that even though our elbows may bleed and sting, our backs may ache, and we may have to cross our legs tightly when we crawl back into the boat, we don't have to be afraid of the ride.

Chapter Thirty-One
The Fly on the Airplane

Twice on that one vacation to California—once going and once coming back—I noticed a fly on my airplane. Two airplanes, and most likely two flies, but both times a fly surprised me by landing on the seat back in front of me.

It wasn't so hard to figure out how the flies got on the planes, but as I watched the first one flit around, landing on people, windows, and overnight bags, I wondered how it might get out. There was really only one way—and that human-sized porthole was only available at certain times for discrete durations.

Touching the Trees

It wasn't until the second fly ended up sharing the on-board lavatory with me, the two of us in the smallest compartment available to humans on the aircraft, both staring into the mirror (granted, the fly was *standing* on it—I can't completely vouch for the staring) that I began to wonder if this fly was trying to tell me something. He was bugging me—in my mind, it was to the exclusion of all the other travelers—and I wanted to know why.

Then I figured it out. I had some unfinished business that I was resisting completing. And that unfinished business was bugging me too. In fact, it was interfering with some very important areas of my personal life. Peter and I had spent parts of our last couple of vacation days talking about the possibility of creating a home and sharing a life together. There was so much about those conversations that felt right. I was quickly approaching the point of not wanting to spend one more day without him as my house and life-mate.

But there was a problem. Thank goodness Peter took the risk of pointing it out to me, coincidentally on the way to the airport, where I met the second fly. He saw that I didn't own my life enough yet to be able to share it with him like it should be shared between two partners. He told me he wouldn't ask me to give until I could give freely. He wouldn't let me go from feeling beholden to my ex-husband to feeling beholden to him. And that he cared enough about my journey that he would help me stay true to my course (which is part of why I fell in love with him in the first place).

He also knew that it was time for me to look my biggest issue full in the face and deal with it, regardless of its impact on our relationship.

See, during this whole transition from being the person I thought I was supposed to be to being the person I *wanted* to be, there was one issue that I alternated between refusing to reflect on and pretending to resolve—neither action actually accomplishing any real reflection or resolution. It was the question of ownership. It was a question that had been buzzing around me, sticking close enough to the periphery of all my other work that I could see it as a nuisance, but not so close that I felt like I had to deal with it immediately. It needed a way out, though. I needed to find a way to close the door on it, finally.

It was the fly on *my* airplane.

Unfortunately, I had a few issues with ownership. First, I had the basic, concrete issue of having very little that had only my name on it as a sole owner. The very definition of ownership is the legal concept of having title to something. But my house had my ex-husband's name on both the title and the mortgage, despite it being quit-claimed to me during the divorce. My car was both registered and titled in those same two names, since I didn't have enough income to support a loan. My personal property was all paid for "by him" using alimony money post-divorce.

Second, my income was derived almost completely from alimony and child support. Sure I brought in a few hundred dollars here and there—enough to pay for some extras for myself and the kids—but if I applied for a credit card, I couldn't list an employer, save myself. I didn't earn any money for my volunteer efforts, certainly, and very little from my book sales or editing jobs. My money was earned by being a stay-home parent married to an income-driven man. And society doesn't often look at that as much more than being on the dole, particularly now that we're not married anymore.

Third, I struggled with owning my emotions. I spent years and years doing one of three things: 1) not allowing myself to feel happiness, sadness, anger, desperation, shame, pride, or anything else along those lines; 2) allowing myself to feel a little bit but not being able to identify the emotion for what it meant; or 3) allowing myself to feel, identifying the emotion, but deciding that it wasn't important. It took me much therapy with Zane to learn how to listen to my emotions and take action based on them.

Finally, I needed to find a way to own myself—my skills, talents, and calling as a writer. I needed to be able to answer the question that I often get and more often dread, "So, what do you do for a living?" with my head high and my heart calm. It was my own decision to pursue my passion rather than a paycheck and I needed to acknowledge and accept that.

So what did I need to do to sweep that fly out of my lavatory and off my plane? How was I going to put that nagging question of ownership where it belonged—outside my line of sight and outside my realm of worry?

I had some thoughts. Regarding the house and the car, I needed to get those things in my name only. Any doubt I had about that was gone. It was already my house in many senses: the down payment was all mine, and every mortgage payment had been made by me. But before I could share it with Peter and his son as part of my family, I needed to have only my name on the title and my name on the mortgage. I needed to spend some amount of time owning that house in all possible ways, not just for all practical purposes. Only then would I be able to invite the two of them inside its walls and, without reservation, call it theirs too.

The car was a little simpler matter, in that it would only take a signature from my ex, along with $20, to transfer title solely to me. Like the house, I was the only one who ever made a payment on it. It was mine the minute I brought it home. It wasn't even something I needed to share with Peter in any legal sense, although I was totally content letting him do with it anything he wanted (which wasn't much because he didn't generally have a lot of need to borrow a smaller vehicle full of pop cans, food wrappers, crayons, stickers, pennies, school papers, sports socks, dust, and crumbs).

But what could I do about the question of owning my income? That was a really hard question for me, especially when I heard at every turn about how I was taking "his" money or how I would feel differently about leeching off of him if I'd been the one supporting the family. It was the myth I'd lived under ever since I gave up my career as a teacher 15 years ago, by mutual agreement, to raise my family: that his money was his money.

I would love to propose to the divorce-focused part of the legal community a different way of looking at the stay-home parent when it comes to divvying up income.

1) What if there was a dollar amount assigned to the "job" of parent?
2) What if I earned, say, minimum wage for every hour I worked?
3) What if that amount of money earned each year was multiplied by the number of years I performed those duties?
4) And what if, at the time of divorce, that total amount was divided by the amount I needed to live off of each month?
5) I would get the money I was owed in the increments I needed in order to survive.

We would have a number—a concrete, limited, fair amount of money that was truly earned and, post-marriage, paid. There wouldn't need to be the "new marriage voids all alimony agreements" clause in divorces—the clause that presupposes, in a very biased, discriminatory way, that a stay-home parent who remarries should be done living off of one spouse because he or she is living off another. It would simply be like being bought out when two business partners disband. It would mean that all stay-home parents own their income as if they worked outside the home.

That system wasn't in place for me in case law, but that doesn't mean I can't believe that I earned every dollar that now comes in the door each month.

Even if I hadn't been the one to get up every night, deal with most of the vomit, all of the carpooling, and every other little tangible and intangible piece of staying home raising kids, just the fact that I gave up a career to perform even half of those duties meant I earned each dollar I get now. He's only funneling to me, through his paycheck, money that is rightfully mine. I need to believe that.

What about my emotions? Well, thankfully I'm well on my way toward owning those. I even had the very clear thought, as I floated on an inflatable raft far up in the Californian mountains and watched two American eagles do a graceful, soaring dance over the lake, that I am happy. I am happy in an unencumbered way, with no strings attached and no expectations placed upon that happiness to last a certain amount of time or exist with a certain intensity.

I was able to identify that happiness and even went one step further. I decided to be all in—to choose the life that I know makes me happy. I drifted on that pillow of air on top of the quiet lake ripples and decided that I trust my emotions enough now to know, with all certainty, how I want to live my life.

Part of how I was able to come to that conclusion is that I've been frighteningly honest with myself and Peter—maybe not always right away, since it sometimes still takes me a little time to work through the process of identification and understanding of my feelings—and he's done the same with me. We've always grown closer as a couple and stronger as individuals. I don't fear that my emotions are "wrong" anymore. They're mine, they're important, and they mean something. Every time, whether they are uncomfortable or not.

As to owning my life as a writer, unashamedly…I'm working on that, word by word. What I realized is that while it may be easy for me to write and I feel called to write, that doesn't mean it's not an important, valuable endeavor. I write nearly every day, certainly quite a bit every week. I have dreams and goals and I work to the best of my ability to achieve them, just like every other artist and every other professional. So I'm kicking the problem of owning myself as a writer out the door with this promise to myself: the next time someone asks me what I do for a living (and the time after that and the time after that) I will say "I'm a writer" without the accompanying "But I don't make much money doing it" or "But mostly I volunteer" or any of the other discounting statements I usually offer.

I was ready to begin the process of owning my life when I decided that I needed to live in a way that was more identity-authentic and emotionally healthy. I took some steps toward living a life I could be proud of when I moved myself and the kids into a new place and divorced. But it took the possibility of expanding my life even more—of being able to share myself with someone that, every day and without question, wants me to be the very best I can be—that gave me the push to capture the airplane fly in my hands, walk it to the exit, and let it go.

Touching the Trees

Chapter Thirty-Two
The Carousel

I used to be scared of funerals and old people. Those fears started when I was young, growing up in a time period when it wasn't proper in my family for kids to be involved in the normal cycle of life—visiting babies in the hospital, watching the old grow older, and letting the sick die. My fears also grew out of an imagination that could contemplate living creatures elsewhere in the universe but couldn't understand how my eyes had opened onto this particular life...and how that meant they could someday be forever shut. Funerals and old people reminded me that I, too, was going to die—which caused me more than one freak-out as a kid and young adult.

It's why I couldn't write my own obituary at Zane's request and why I can't bear to think of that last moment and when it might come.

My first important memory of death was when I was about eight years old. My mother's family came to visit—my grandparents, an uncle who was 14, and two aunts who were 16 and 18. I recall that it was in late summer or early fall. I remember that my grandfather, who almost never spoke, was in line with me to get a hamburger fresh off the grill. While we waited, he gently tapped my dirty bare foot with his dress shoe and smiled a very rare smile just at me. Even as young as I was, it felt like a special moment between me, the oldest granddaughter, and my grandpa.

Then, within a few hours, he had a heart attack and died in my younger brother's bed. He was 54.

And, according to my mom, I was "too young" to go to the funeral.

Since that time I've been to other funerals, of course. I went to the funeral of one of my very best high school friends, who was killed in a car accident during Christmas break of our freshman year in college. I went to the funeral of a baby who died of SIDS just 18 months after his older sister died of anencephaly. I also went to the wake of a former co-worker of my mother's and had to stand at the casket and answer the grieving widow (a virtual stranger) when she asked in teary seriousness, "Doesn't he look good?"

But a funeral is just an event. It's an experience that can be shaped by the tenor of the mourning and one's relationship with the decedent. It may not be pleasant, but that's because it's usually centered around sadness and longing.

My favorite funerals, if it's not too improper to say that, have been ones that have turned into boisterous, laughing family reunions with tales spun and expanded upon until the whole event became part of the fabric of memories. My wholesale fear of funerals has lessened because sometimes they've opened doors on relationships that might have otherwise been walled off or stuck in superficiality.

Attending a funeral is a whole different thing than spending time with a person who's old and dying, though. Like many young people, I used to resist visiting with elderly relatives. A couple of the most uncomfortable nights of my life were spent having a sleepover at my great-grandparents' house. Once I slept in the recliner (and, even as a kid had the worst backache I'd ever experienced) and once I slept in one of the twin beds in their bedroom (which was not uncomfortable, but was certainly confusing). I don't remember having an ounce of fun and took the expectation of having a bad time around old people into my adult years.

Later, when I was newly married, we were pressured quite relentlessly to visit my husband's grandparents. The pressure increased exponentially after our first child was born until we finally buckled and visited them when my son was about eight weeks old. At first it was awful and awkward, just as I thought it would be. I wasn't sure how to talk to an old man who simply stared from his chair in the corner. I knew I should help my son's great-grandma (who had paralysis from a bout with polio) prepare dinner but I used my newborn as an excuse to stay planted, safely, in the land of the young and away from the small talk of the old.

But then I looked at my son (who was staring up at me from the floor) and at the grandpa (who was contemplating a bowl of applesauce) and realized that they were at the two ends of the mortality spectrum and, in reality, weren't so different from one another. As one of them got closer to eating real food, the other was approaching liquids. As one was nearing the time of using a walker to learn steps, the other needed that support to steady his weakening legs. Then I understood that the staring coming from the corner wasn't the silent judgment of a grumpy German. It was the glazed gaze of an intelligent man being faced with a life full of nuances that were suddenly just beyond his grasp. In very base terms, they both needed someone to change their diapers—which made both of them need caretaking and compassion.

It was just about then that I quit being afraid of old people. It wasn't that man's choice to become infirm and dependent—it was just the natural order of things. Just as I couldn't resent or be afraid of my baby needing me, I couldn't resent or be afraid of my elderly anymore.

But I was still afraid of my own life turning into a series of hours spent in uncomprehending frustration. I was still afraid of wasting what might be the one life I'd been given. I was still afraid of dying.

Which brings me to the toy store.

In the middle of what seems like nowhere, on the southern Minnesota side of the Mississippi River, is a store called Lark Toys. The store is an oddity—part museum, part toy store, part ice cream shop, and part mini golf course. How it stays in business is a bit beyond my limited marketing sense to understand.

To make Lark Toys even more interesting, though, is that at the center of that roadside attraction is a beautiful, hand-carved, hand-painted wooden carousel.

Sitting in the dining area to cool off from a hot Sunday drive, I had a chance to soak in the life-like details of the monkeys hanging off the giraffe's neck, the baby otters crawling all over their mama, the ostrich pulling a cart full of giant, cracked eggs, and the fish overflowing the pelican's mouth. Just like the information placard said, chisel marks were visible underneath the paint and those etchings seemed to both absorb and reflect the summer light coming through the windows.

At about half past the hour, kids I hadn't noticed before streamed in from the mini golf course and the toy store. They handed off melting ice cream cups to grandparents and grabbed their parents' hands. It was time for a ride on the centerpiece of the operation.

As the carousel started turning, I could see animals I hadn't seen from my stationary position at the table. Most intriguing to me was the flamingo that had one leg tucked up underneath her body but whose other leg, which I assumed she would be "standing" on, seemed to be missing. Every time the flamingo passed me I tried to figure out if she was really missing a leg or if I was just unable to see it through the spinning maze of other figures.

After a few minutes, the carousel stopped and all the kids and parents stepped off the wooden platform and back to their picture-snapping relatives and liquefied sherbet. Not one of them was crying or afraid. They'd had a blast.

A little later, on my way out the door of Lark Toys, back to the heat of the drive and my own busy world, I thought about how fortunate I was to have experienced such a magnificent work of art in such an unlikely place. Then I thought about how being on that carousel could be compared to a life well-lived—more joy than frustration, more fulfillment than regret. Finally, I thought that if a life's ride's going to end anyway, then the best way to enjoy it is to absorb and reflect all the beauty that can be found during the short time it runs.

Don't get me wrong—I'm not done trying to make sense of why I'm who I am and not a train conductor honking his way through small towns, or an owner of a small toy store on Highway 61, or even some other woman with three kids who's trying in vain to be on time for carpools in some other state's suburbia. Despite being able to find joy in funerals and understanding in the caretaking of my old relatives, I'm still afraid of dying.

But I have a small sense of relief that when my eyes close someday for good and the light that is my own particular conscience is forever extinguished (hopefully at some very advanced age), my life will have been lovingly crafted, just like the carousel.

We all have the chance (and maybe even the obligation) to put that much effort into creating beautiful lives for ourselves. Certainly, we can craft parts of those lives for other people to enjoy, but we also need to remember to pour our energy into chiseling a work of art that *we* can enjoy. We can make a life that's free of fear that our own personal flamingo doesn't have another leg to stand on. We can make a life that is *ours*.

Touching the Trees

Chapter Thirty-Three
Nine or None

One warm August evening, when the stars aligned and book club landed on a Friday when I didn't have my kids or any other obligations or plans, I went. Book clubs, in general, are anything and everything portrayed by society and husbands. They are social occasions, sometimes including actual book talk, that more often than not also include wine and food. But they are also a time and place of connection, laughter, and exploration. My book club, specifically, is a group of women (mostly neighbors) who have raised children together, battled all kinds of cancer together, lost and gained a couple of husbands and pounds, and met for years.

I used to live for going to book club. It was my one guaranteed night "out" during the time when I was home all day, week after week, with the kids. I would dress up in my cleanest appliqued sweat suit or comfortable jeans (that is until a well-intentioned member pulled me aside and suggested, gently, that I didn't really have to dress like my mother quite yet) and walk to a neighbor's house, carrying a bowl of cream cheese dip (cream cheese and salsa, cream cheese and corn, cream cheese and ranch dressing, cream cheese and fruit…) or a bag of peanut M&Ms as my contribution to the evening's menu.

But then I moved away and it was harder to get back to those friends and that connection. Sometimes it was hard because the three mile drive seemed too reckless after a night of drinking; sometimes it was hard because of my kids' hockey/lacrosse/social schedule. Eventually, I became busy making new friends in the new neighborhood. So for a few years I rarely attended. Then I moved again and found that it was a little easier to make the decision to go.

So I went to book club that August night. Against my intellectual values, I didn't read the book (for the second or third time in a row—how embarrassing). Against my body's wish for a nap and a warm blanket (I was in the throes of a couple different upper respiratory and ENT infections), I put on some capris, bound up my hair into a ponytail, swiped on some eyeliner, and showed up without an appetizer or a beverage.

After a tasty dinner of steak and chicken kabobs, with side dishes of flavored rice and Brussels sprouts (and the requisite couple of drinks, despite my stuffiness and interminable cough), we all convened in the living room to talk about the book. But before we started our book discussion, one of the women posed to the group something she'd been asked on vacation the week before…

"Nine or none?"

Everyone's first response was, of course, "Nine or none what?"

The answer: "Kids. If you had to choose between having nine children or none, what would you pick?"

Huh. While I thought about my answer, other people piped in with their thoughts.

The woman who is one of eight children herself, although one of her brothers died from leukemia as a child, said nine. The woman who is married to a man she's still giddily in love with after nearly twenty years of marriage said nine. The woman from a mid-sized Italian family, but who only has two kids of her own, said nine. Most of the Catholics said nine.

But more interesting to me were the ones who said none. The empath/school psychologist whose kids are wonderful free spirits (but whose angry ex-husband had been really scary at times) said none. The professor at a Christian college with two very intelligent sons (one of whom has had more than his share of drug problems and the other who has had great success in the arts) said none. The woman who never says one bad word about her husband or her nearly grown children said none.

When it got to me (after circling around the room a couple of times), I copped out and said it depended. Of course, the other women quickly reminded me that my answer went against the point of the game.

So, what if I had no children? Sure, I'd be doing something completely different and maybe I'd have some measurable success in terms of retirement accounts or status. Maybe I'd be living a writer's dream—a seaside villa, a wait staff, cats all over the place, tremendous intellectual repartee with other artists, many lovers or maybe just one devoted companion, travel plans, a cute little car.... Or maybe I'd be slogging through my days at an ad agency, hoping that the next middle manager or new client was a single man or one with wife trouble. Maybe I'd be filling my nights with television. Maybe I'd be filling them with sleep. Maybe I'd be filling them with exercise class or sex. Who knew?

And what if I had nine? That's where the "depends" came in.

I have three now. Barring divine intervention or a second coming, I will only ever have three. Three have been plenty to fill up my child-bearing years. My three haven't been difficult to raise—but neither have they been pieces of cake. My oldest was a terrible sleeper and struggled with Attention Deficit Disorder during elementary and middle school. My middle child has always been determined, hard-headed, even bossy. My youngest has both a sleep issue (really, she'll sleep in her own bed someday, right?) and the same bossiness as her brother but with the added element of perfected whining.

As a mother, I struggled against the societal expectations of a "stay-home parent" for most of the time I was married and continue to feel like I don't have the best handle on routines—meal times, bedtimes, school days, sports carpools, discipline, and chores. So, in terms of sheer capacity for taking care of children, I might already be at my limit.

But...what if I'd had a parenting partner who was more compatible with me—more willing to deprive himself of sleep too, more willing to share meal preparation and vomit cleanup? What if I'd had a husband who valued my role as something more than just a way to facilitate his corporate climb? What if the father of my children loved both me and them in ways that made us know we were unquestioningly cherished? In that case, I can tell you I definitely wouldn't have had none. I might just have had nine.

When I decided I was done having children, which was sometime during my last pregnancy, I remember feeling very sure that after this one I did not want to go through the exhaustion and mind-numbing daily work of taking care of another baby. I knew from experience that I would be mostly on my own and I didn't think I could do it a fourth time.

But I was willing to have a third because…well, because I wanted to try to do it all better than I had with my other two children. I wanted to have a baby knowing that my perspective would be different since it was my last one. I wanted to seek joy in being the mother of a baby. And that part worked very well. I felt better about getting up at night because I knew that my sleeplessness had an end date. I felt better going through potty-training because I'd soon be forever done with diapers. I felt relief when she went to school because I could sense my world opening and easing up.

The one thing I didn't anticipate, though, now eight years later, is that my very firm decision to be finished having children (cemented with not just one, but two tubal surgeries) would be challenged simply because I'm with someone that I crave parenting with. I watch Peter with his own child and with my children and know that he is the father with whom I wish I could now create life. I can almost feel his hand on my swelling belly and hear him easing out of bed to comfort a whimpering newborn before I completely wake up. I wish he could give those things to me—those small gestures that mean so much.

But even more, I wish I could give him the chance to parent another child of his own without the anguish of dealing with his ex-wife and her manipulation of his son's feelings. He really is man who was made to be a father. I also wish I could give all of our children another sibling to tease, be frustrated by, care for, and love for a lifetime.

The hard reality is that I probably wouldn't have done well with nine children, even if Peter and I were able to have those children together now. I like sleep and time alone with my thoughts too much to devote large chunks of every day to caring for children anymore. The housekeeping and meals that would go along with all those people living together would be impossible for me to handle (I can barely do it for three kids and myself as it is).

But I also miss the child or children I'll never have with Peter. I miss them terribly. I miss the experiences he and I don't share and often wonder who we might be today if we were side-by-side back then, going through the fiery relationship initiation of child-bearing. I grieve for the child that lives in my heart and in my imagination but who will never nuzzle my breast.

I'm sad that we won't have that most permanent of lifelong bonds to one another.

You can't make a baby out of nothing, though. So we'll do our best with the children who already need us and love us. Unlike the first times around, our new family won't start with the birth of a baby. It will start with the birth of a commitment to each other and each other's children. And our number will never be either nine or none.

It will always be four—four children that we're eternally grateful for.

Chapter Thirty-Four
Strings

One of my favorite scenes in *The Sound of Music* is when Maria and the Von Trapp children put on a puppet show for the Captain and the Baroness. The marionettes prance around the stage, acting out "The Lonely Goatherd" while Maria and the kids sing all the parts.

Even though I have known for a long time that the puppets were actually manipulated by professional puppeteers, it still amazes me that the strings didn't get tangled beyond extrication. Four or more strings per puppet? Special levers for eyes and eyebrows and mouths? I'm always awed and amazed at the complexity of those puppets.

Not early enough in my life, I figured out that relationships always have some kind of complex system of strings too. There are the strings that bind us to each other—ones that are common experiences, memories, affections, and hopes. These are our tie-offs as we climb the proverbial mountains and figuratively jump out of the planes of our daily lives. We need these strings to feel safely connected to the people we care about and love. We need to provide strength and heft to these strings if we want to maintain loving, healthy relationships.

Then there are the other kinds of strings. These strings are marionette controls gone wrong. They are tangled and stuck in our hair or on our ankles or near our hearts like Taser wires on unruly criminals—delivering jolts of pain and tying up our reflexes and appendages until we can't freely move or feel. They are strings of conditional love.

During my life, the ties that bound me to important people, like my parents and my husband, became secondary to the ties that controlled. I felt like so much of those relationships was conditional—if I behaved in a way that made their lives easier, then they was easier to get along with, which I interpreted as love. If I behaved in a way that caused them anxiety or frustration, then they became difficult and bossy and I felt unloved. So I trained myself to avoid conflict with people I cared about because I didn't like having to defend myself against emotional whiplash, time and time again. If-then (and all that occurred during the hyphen) was some not-so-silly string—a convoluted, nebulous, and sticky concoction that created co-dependency instead of balanced relationships.

So when I began this journey toward a new, stronger life, I vowed never to allow myself to be strung up like that again—and I vowed never to put conditions or strings on anyone else either.

When I began seeing Peter, we agreed to come to the table free and clear of expectations, demands, and consequences. There would be no if-then for us because we'd both lived in relationships decimated by those types of strings and were determined not to live that way again.

It was a good plan, until the tiptoeing and the string-avoidance became a string of its own. It became a condition that we not put conditions on each other. And I worried that if I needed to set some boundaries, then I'd break that rule of our relationship.

One of our first and most emotionally-charged issues as a couple is that two of his longtime friends (friends Peter have thought of as his best friends for a long time) have been acting in ways that feel hurtful. They chose to remain friends with my ex-husband, who's their neighbor, often to the exclusion of us. They once even texted us that the "coast is clear" after turning us down for a night out so they could spend it with him instead. Then they expected that we would drop what we were doing to run over and to see them.

In their defense, they have missed hanging out with Peter; they've missed having things the way they always were. After a while, though, Peter felt like they put conditions on him, like "spend as much time with us as you used to or we'll find a new friend." It's possible they felt like Peter put conditions on them, too, like "don't be friends with Jennifer's ex-husband or I won't spend time with you."

Then I muddied up the waters by telling Peter that I didn't care to put much effort into my own relationship with them because I didn't like how they were treating him or how they'd taken my ex-husband's side. I worried that he would think I was putting conditions on his relationship with him by defining mine—that he would feel like he had to choose between them and me.

Fortunately, Peter and I never got to that point of putting those ultimate conditions on each other, like me saying "I don't want you to hang out with them" or him saying "You have to hang out with them."

Regardless, it still felt like there were strings all over the place.

Our second weightiest issue is Peter's custody agreement with his ex-wife. Over the course of many years of knowing him, I saw him give in to her schedule demands almost every time they had contact with each other. She would threaten, disparage, manipulate, and bully him until he would forego even more of his limited parenting time with his son. Anytime he attempted to stand up to her, she criticized his parenting style, his choice of a partner, and how he spent his money. She even made numerous attempts at turning Peter's son against him, his family, and his friends.

After Peter and I decided we wanted to share a life together, her hold on him became a very real issue for me. I didn't want to worry about her messing up my schedule with my children or messing up my kids' relationships with Peter's son. I wanted her to stop hurting the man I cared about. I also wanted to know that he was strong enough to make her stop.

So I suggested, not always so gently, that he take her to court to remedy the fact that she was in violation of the divorce decree every week and had been for ten years. I strategized scenarios and spent many hours researching how he could succeed using the legal system and win back time with his son. I offered to go to court with him and prepare all the documentation ahead of time.

I even went so far as to tell Peter that I didn't think we could move in together until he took care of his problem with her.

I honestly thought I was setting a boundary. It turns out I was doing the one thing I'd promised him I wouldn't do—setting a condition. I was attaching a string.

The problem was that I thought it was a string of love and caring. I believed that if he grasped onto my ultimatum, it would free him of her control. If he would comply with my demands for a little while, he would eventually see that he was better off that way.

Huh.

I also thought that setting boundaries with him wouldn't feel so much like an if-then.

After several months of me pushing him about his friends, his ex-wife, and his custody schedule, Peter finally had enough. We were sitting at a bar, having a beer and talking about our friends and our future. The subject of his son came up and I started my usual line of questioning about when he was going to file the papers.

Then he surprised me. He took my hand, looked me in the eyes, and said, "I think that's more your agenda than mine. I'm okay with how things are. I may not like it all the time, but *I* can live with it. The real question is, can you?"

I sat there for a second until I realized he was right. It *was* more my agenda than his. These were *my* conditions on him. He needed me to love him for who he was right then— not who he might be if he stood up to his friends and his ex-wife.

It was time for me to let go of the strings I wanted to put on him and enjoy the strings we already had—our trust in and affection for each other.

In *The Sound of Music*, Captain Von Trapp is a lonely widower who is engaged to marry a woman of social stature, the Baroness. It's an engagement based less on love than on political arrangement. The Baroness has her conditions: among other things, if the children are around, then they must be seen and not heard. If they are to be the step-children of a Baroness, then they must act like royalty.

But problems arise for the Captain when he realizes that he's actually falling in love with the children's' governess, Maria. She provides strings of connection to his children and to his love of music, rather than setting conditions on everyone's behavior. And that's the life the Captain really wants.

I know what it's like to be the Captain and have other people place expectations and conditions on me. I didn't like it and was determined to go nowhere near a condition again.

Then I almost became the Baroness.

It's been hard to find an answer to the question of conditions/strings vs. boundaries. What I thought was a boundary—asking Peter to fix the problems with his ex-wife—was a condition. What some may think is a condition—me wanting to maintain some distance from Peter's friends—might be a legitimate boundary.

I just know that we have to be careful about trying to change or control others in our lives. If that's what we're doing, we're probably attaching strings of conditional love. If what we're doing instead is trying to change our own behavior, then we might just be setting healthy boundaries for ourselves.

Touching the Trees

Chapter Thirty-Five
Weed Killer

Many years ago, in the middle of summer, I was deep into my annual battle against garden weeds. I'd put in a large perennial garden on a hill that had formerly been ten tons of crushed rock and was determined to make it into a lush, layered, flowering paradise. Because I chose not to put down any weed barrier between the new dirt and the new mulch, though, my challenge was to let the Miracle-Gro work on the plants I wanted, and get the weed killer to work on the plants I didn't.

So one day I grabbed a new bottle of weed killer from the garage and started to squirt. Then I tried some more. Nothing came out; the nozzle was broken. Luckily, I still had an empty bottle in the garage so I could solve the problem of full bottle/broken nozzle meets empty bottle/working nozzle. What I did next says a lot about how my brain works.

If you're thinking, "This is easy—you take the working nozzle and put it on the full bottle," you'd be using a part of your brain that I haven't fully developed, even now.

What I did was take off the nozzles of both bottles, proceed, very carefully, to pour the weed killer from one bottle to the other, and replace the original nozzles. Problem solved—full bottle/working nozzle. In retrospect, lots of extra work.

Since that time I've had thousands of conflicts to work through and logistical problems to solve. From the daily decisions around getting the kids from point A to point B to the bigger decisions around starting a new life, I've made them and generally solved all the minor problems. But sometimes those decisions have taken more work than they should. Sometimes, if it's a particularly difficult decision, I throw in some extra steps as a way to avoid potential (or real) conflict. I pour very carefully instead of just switching the nozzle.

I had this problem a lot when I first decided to leave my marriage. I took baby steps when I wanted to run and engaged in dialogues when I just wanted to hold up my hand and say, "Enough, already!" I tiptoed and listened and participated in late-night autopsies of the relationship and of my role as a "good" mother. I sat through hours of serial television because it was "our" favorite show and my husband didn't want to face that he might have to watch it without me. I agreed to a methodology of telling the kids and other people about the impending divorce. I also agreed to limit my own support system, even though having a smaller circle made it just that much more difficult to navigate my thoughts and feelings.

I was afraid of being judged as heartless and stupid. I was afraid of being labeled a bad mother and a money-grubber. I was especially anxious about being thought of as a cheater—because I wanted him to understand that I wasn't leaving him for someone else. I was leaving him for me.

That fear of being judged hasn't gone away, even though the marriage has. I still take the long way around decisions in order to avoid judgment. I still pour when I should just get the job done.

Here's another case in point. When I started dating Peter I worried about the timing of embarking on a new relationship. I worried for myself because I was still enmeshed in the particular crazy that comes from extracting oneself from a long-term emotionally manipulative situation. I worried that I wasn't standing square enough on my own two feet to begin dancing with someone else.

More than that, I cared a lot (way too much, most likely) what other people thought. My fear of judgment—that fear that had always made me take the walking path around difficult decisions instead of the bridge through the center—took up a lot of my first few months with Peter. Our relationship grew into a beautiful, supportive way of being, but we hid it from friends, family, and our kids because I was still afraid of being judged. Truth be told, we put a lot of extra work into making "us" okay for everyone else.

We agonized over who should know and when. We tempered our excitement about being together if there was someone around that we weren't sure liked the idea.

In our defense regarding the kids, it was important for them to be kept in the dark for a while longer than everyone else. I'd read enough about kids and divorce to know that they didn't need to have another change thrown at them while we were all still in the midst of sorting out the major upheaval they were experiencing. So I don't regret keeping my kid time and my Peter time separate for a few months. But I do regret that we spent so many hours worrying what some neighbor or friend or ex-spouse or stranger thought about us dating.

Once we felt comfortable with our relationship, though, we relaxed and enjoyed our time together with the kids, our friends, and each other.

After many months of growing our relationship, Peter and I decided to take a motorcycle drive to northern Minnesota. During that trip, on a stunningly clear, cool morning on a road called the Gunflint Trail, Peter pulled the motorcycle over to an empty wayside and we walked up to a small lake. While we were there, Peter asked me to do him the honor of agreeing to spend the rest of our lives together.

I said yes with overwhelming joy and no hesitation. It was the most beautiful proposal I could have imagined—because there was no expectation, no subtext, no doubt. It was just us, the birds, and a glassy lake.

Perfection.

A little ways down the road, though, after the tremendous importance of that moment sank in, some questions came up. Questions like: What did we just agree to? Are people going to think it's too soon? What should we tell the kids? How will our friends and family react when we explain that we won't be having a formal, legal wedding but might celebrate with something more casual and personal? Will they label and judge us? We know how we feel about each other, but….

So we talked about all of those things during the rest of that day. We beat the issue to a bloody pulp, as Peter became fond of saying on that trip. We tried to anticipate what the kids' reactions would be and whether or not our respective exes would try to interfere in our new life together. We worried about messing up our extended families' plans for next summer. We stumbled around whom to tell, when, how, and why. Frankly, we weren't even sure *what* to tell anyone. Were we engaged? We didn't know.

In all of that discussion, I got further mired in my twin fears of being judged and of getting stuck in the girlfriend/fiancée/wife/stepmother box. I wanted to commit to this wonderful man, but not to the exclusion of continuing on my personal journey of growth.

I got mad at myself for getting so caught up in fear management, but it didn't stop me from going there anyway. In our society, "getting engaged" sets into motion a whole series of events that can get out of control quickly. That's why bridal planning guides sell by the millions every year. So many questions: Can we see the ring? When's the date? Where's it going to be? Who are the attendants? Who's invited? Why aren't you making it legal? And in our case, so few answers correspond to what's considered normal: No ring right now. We don't know. We don't know. Don't know that either. Haven't thought about it. Because of my divorce stipulations....

We weren't even sure we were engaged, since we weren't planning to be legally married. Maybe we were going steady, but in a really grown-up way. Regardless, we felt like we'd made a commitment to each other and we also felt like we might want to share that news with our closest family and friends.

However, every step of a betrothal has a societally prescribed set of expectations and if a couple doesn't subscribe to those expectations, other people get a little anxious. When other people get anxious, I feel judged. So Peter and I spent the 48 hours after that life-affirming moment pouring answers from one bottle into another bottle. And we did it with great, painstaking deliberation.

In all honesty, maybe it would be easier for me to not care what other people think if I didn't fear the boxes so much. Maybe it's a catch-22 in that I fear the boxes because I care too much about what other people think. Maybe I just needed to be honest with myself and Peter and acknowledge that I didn't want to label our relationship. I don't know.

What I do know is this: Years ago I didn't intentionally make the weed killer bottle swap harder on myself—it's just how I'm wired to think. But today I'm still wired to make some decisions more work than they need to be and I suspect that it will be a struggle for a long time. One thing I've figured out, though, is that I only make decisions hard for myself when I try to ignore my feelings. I only skirt the issues when I don't want to face them head-on.

I'm just grateful that I finally understand that we can all replace the weeds of self-doubt with the quiet serenity of a confident life. There is so much more power in being honest with ourselves.

Touching the Trees

Chapter Thirty-Six
Water Weight

Ahh, it's that time of the month again. I'm not talking about my period, either. I'm talking about the week before. Labeled PMS or pre-menstrual syndrome, it's become a catch phrase for anyone who's moody or bloated but usually describes the few days before a woman's period. My PMS announces its presence with a loud crunch—the sound of an unsuspecting someone else eating a chip or a carrot or an apple…or, to be honest with you, even a chocolate chip in a bowl of ice cream. Like a well-tuned antenna, I can pick up a mouth noise from anywhere in the house and, if my reaction is one of white-hot, irrational anger, then I know it's That Week.

Occasionally (thank goodness not every time), my PMS week also includes an unbelievable amount of water weight gain. We're talking pounds and pounds of water, sloshing around in my ankles, making my fingers look like beer brats, and distending my abdomen to the point where I'm pretty sure it's either going to be a period or a ten-pounder coming out of me within 5-7 days.

For some reason (and let's not say it's age, ok?) I've had a little more trouble lately battling the water weight. It may just be that I eat salt like I breathe air; it could be that I don't sweat nearly enough. It could also be that I ate a lot of bar food during those three months I spent nearly every other Saturday or Sunday on the back of a motorcycle. Regardless of the reason, I've got a watermelon's worth of it in me and it's ticking me off, almost as much as my kids and their friends eating popcorn with their mouths open does…from two floors away.

One month I tried a few water pills—which worked for about a half day and then seemed to have an opposite effect. I also tried to eat some raw vegetables without salt and actually succeeded a couple of times. Turns out, cucumbers, tomatoes and sugar snap peas can taste okay without it. Who knew?

I went for a walk, sat out at a hot pool, and drank more water. I had one glass of wine instead of two for dinner and managed to order White Castle for my kids and not eat any…except three or four fries. I also got my period.

But I was still bloated. I was so full of water that my smallish breasts jiggled like they hit the big time and became B cups. My feet still felt like I was walking on marshmallows and I was nearly convinced that, period notwithstanding, I might just need to call up the producers of TLC's *I Didn't Know I Was Pregnant* and let them know what hospital I'd be rushing to.

I had some serious water shedding to take care of.

In all of my moodiness and crabbiness during the most recent past episode, when I wasn't stuffing my face with chips and M&Ms, I had time to reflect on some of the other things I wanted to do, besides install drains in the backs of my knees and run my hands through a fondant press. I wanted to get rid of a few things: the elliptical machine I will never use, the good china that's never been unboxed, the kitchen table with only three chairs, and the sleeper/sofa/sectional that's free to a good home—or even a bad home, as long as it's out of my basement.

I also needed to fix a few things: the electrical system in my house that blows light bulbs like July 4th fireworks every two months, the bare spots in my yard, the paint color in my daughter's room, and the wireless router that was invaded by a colony of ants…then drenched in bug killer.

Touching the Trees

As Peter and I discussed in more detail the option of sharing one house, the lists of things to get rid of and fix increased exponentially and expensively. There was a lot to do. And it's that list—the list of how to make two houses into one home, four kids into one unit, two adults into one couple—that led me to an even more important list.

Call it a "bucket list." It's all of the things I want to do to complete my transformation from a fear-based life into one that is whole, complete and ready for sharing.

When I felt emotionally suffocated and frustrated before, I had some vague goals that were less of a bucket list and more of a linty, wrinkled Target receipt that had been scribbled on, left in a pants pocket, and run through the washing machine for fifteen years. They were things I should have accomplished much earlier in my life and seemed more catch-up than moving-forward:

1) Live on my own
2) Raise my kids without depending on (and being disappointed by) their other parent
3) Learn to pay my bills on time, save money, and survive financially
4) Make decisions based, when appropriate, on what I need or want

Most of that list I worked very hard on and (I can say with some level of confidence) completed. Now it was time to dive a little deeper. What was it I needed to do—or what did I just plain *want* to do—before this particular transition was complete? What were the things that were left—the trees I still wanted to throw my arms around and kiss goodbye? Here was a new list:

1) Travel alone—figuratively, literally, and regularly—to places where I could spend time in reflection or in a bar or both
2) Support myself and my kids with income derived independent of alimony
3) Sell my books
4) Learn to ride a motorcycle
5) Get that ever-elusive tattoo
6) Use my enduring fears of judgment, failure, *and success* as motivators and not as excuses for complacency.

Number 6—that might just be the key to completing this journey.

I kept hoping to eliminate judgment from my life—using my new freedom to transition away from being a person who constantly felt guilty for "messing up" or for making someone else unhappy or uncomfortable. I gave whole decades over to being the person who replayed party conversations, check-out line encounters, marital spats, and personal requests and then found myself lacking in politeness, considerateness, and selflessness. I let fear of judgment be my guide and guilt be my pre-emptive punishment for far too long...so long that it was almost my permanent way of being. But the last couple of years have shown me that judgment isn't really a reflection on *me*. It's a reflection on the person doing the judging. It's okay to be confident in my decisions.

I used my fear of failure as a justification for status quo for a long time, too. When I worried that I wouldn't be able to "make it" on my own without depending financially on someone else, I tended to take fewer risks. I looked through piles of uncompleted manuscripts, lists of household projects, and closets of unmatching linens and became nervous that at some point (like when my alimony and child support run out) I wouldn't be able to support myself and would lose much of what I currently had. So I chose to sit tight and not invest in the future in order to hold on to what was already in my pocket. Then I remembered (and was constantly reminded by the people who love me) that the only real failure is in not trying.

Fear of success was my other enduring fear—and it's one that wasn't easy to talk about. I've been afraid of succeeding my whole life. I was one of those kids that did the minimum amount of work necessary to get decent grades. I wasn't one who had to have straight As, even though I probably could have. I earned the coveted position of concertmistress for my city-wide youth orchestra, but didn't work hard enough to shine—just hard enough not to fail. I was the number one women's golfer on my high school team but choked in every tournament. To this day, I'm not sure why I was so afraid of success, except that I didn't want to deal with all the possible changes that could occur as a result of success. I thought the pressure on me would increase even more if I became really good at something.

But back to my original problem—I have a little something to shed. I think most of us do. Carrying around a list of "un-dones" is the same as carrying around the water weight women are sometimes cursed with. If we've set goals that are important to achieve, then we need to start achieving them. Otherwise, the whole point of a transition from there to *here* is pointless. We'll never get from here to *there*, either.

Now, thanks to a cup of coffee, 44 ounces of diet soda and a salt-free lunch, I also (finally and mercifully) have one more very important thing to take care of. So if you'll excuse me….

Touching the Trees

Chapter Thirty-Seven: Afterword
Touching the Trees, Part 2

Shortly before this book went to press, I sat in Zane's office—in my usual spot (his loveseat) on the usual day (Wednesday) at the usual time (11:00 am).

That particular session was mostly taken up with speedy accounts of happy busy things (the near-completion of this book being one of them) and some lingering doubts of the usual confidence variety.

With only about twenty minutes to go, we decided to try hypnosis/guided meditation as a new way to help me overcome the residual tickles of anxiety that still plagued me during times of conflict. I wasn't sure what Zane had planned, but I trusted that I'd feel better when we were finished.

Oh, boy, did I.

At Zane's prompting, I closed my eyes and held my hands quiet in my lap. As he talked, I pictured the top of a staircase. Since it could be any type of staircase, this particular one had gilded risers and rails, with plush red carpet on each step and a wall full of oil portraits and landscape paintings on its left. Slowly I descended the staircase, feeling my bare feet sink into the silent cushion of each step.

When I got to the bottom, though, there was no ballroom, no hallway, and no door. Instead, the plush carpet transformed into cool, flat stepping stones, ribboned with moss, which led to a dry dirt path in the middle of a woods.

I looked around. There was only one path to take, winding though it was, and as I walked, it led me deeper into the forest dappled with blinks of sunlight and the shush of an early autumn breeze.

Along the way, I reached out to the trees on either side of the path. Some, like the birches, were taut and smooth. Others, like the giant elms, were cut with rough rivers of bark as deep as my fingers.

My walk led me to a stand of quaking aspens that were already hinting yellow and orange. They asked me to listen, so I did.

Here's what one said:

"Our purpose, my dear, is to root deeply, grow strong, and give. It's our nature as trees to do these things; it will forever be our nature to do these things."

Another: "You are one of us and always have been. It is *your* nature to seek sustenance from your grounding, all the while reaching your stronging arms to the sky. You also give—sometimes shade, sometimes fruit, and sometimes fire."

"Like us, you are beautiful," they all whispered. "Like us, you are free."

A nearby elm brushed the top of my head. "We cannot, any of us, stay growing, though. Sometimes we must rest. When we rest, we slow down, thicken our saps, and release our leaves. Then we sleep. That is our nature, too.

"You sometimes need to rest, too. But to do that, you need to release the leaves of your discontent and worry, of your mistakes and your sorrow.

"You don't need them anymore."

The aspen spoke again. "Because remember this: Where the discarded leaves once lived, new ones will emerge. It is these new ones that will bring us all to life again and sustain our growth and strength for another season."

With that, my companions gathered me close, touching me, too.

"You have what it takes," they whispered.

Touching the Trees

I stepped back onto the dry dirt path and retraced my steps to the staircase. At the first step, a handful of leaves fluttered from my fingers. As the steps ascended and once more became the soft red plush of my dream-state castle, I felt a cape of leaves floating behind me, untied and falling away from my shoulders.

>I went there and I came back.
>Now I'm home.

Touching the Trees

Questions for Reflection

Chapter 1 (Bad Things and Braveheart): How can you expand yourself? What can you do outside your comfort zone just to prove to yourself that you can? Why might that be important to do?

Chapter 2 (My Cousin Betsy): Is there someone in your life that might be worth reaching out to? Is it possible to have unconditional love? Who is your favorite family member?

Chapter 3 (Old Ladies): What kind of old lady or old man do you want to be? How can you get there? If you had to write your obituary, what would it say?

Chapter 4 (Labels and Boxes): Has someone else labeled you in a way that doesn't fit? Have you done that to yourself? Are there any boxes you want to step out of? If, even now, you could be anything, what would it be? Who would you be?

Chapter 5 (Diamond Rings): What do you do when someone wants something from you that you don't want to give? How does that feel? Do you ever put your needs behind someone else's? When is that okay to do?

Chapter 6 (Touching the Trees, Part 1): What traditions or behavior patterns do you have around saying goodbye? Is it hard for you to say it? In what ways might you "touch the trees" to greet a new person or situation?

Chapter 7 (Abortion and the Egg Farmer's Daughter): What has been your hardest decision to make? Do you regret it or do you believe in your decision? Is it possible for you to turn an unhappy situation into a positive?

Chapter 8 (Arrows): What causes you to have negative thoughts about yourself? How far down do your arrows go? Using a time that brought you down, can you reframe your thoughts to become up arrows?

Chapter 9 (Battleship): Is there a destructive pattern in how you relate to some people? How can you break that?

Chapter 10 (Yeses and Nos): How are you a yes person? How are you a no person? Is there one you wish you were more of?

Chapter 11 (Mine): What is yours and why? Do you deserve what you have?

Chapter 12 (Mirrors): Who do you see in your mirror? Do you like yourself? Are you making decisions you are proud of?

Chapter 13 (Plastic Bags): Is there anyone or anything that is suffocating you emotionally? How might you pull off the plastic bag that covers you?

Chapter 14 (The Doorway Out): Do you need a doorway out? If so, what might it be?

Chapter 15 (Traveling by Anger): Do you stay angry and hold grudges? Try letting go of one frustration—tell yourself that it can't control you anymore. How does that feel?

Chapter 16 (Thunder and Silence): Are there any cycles in your life that you're ready to break? What choices can you make to change the usual course of events?

Chapter 17 (The Replacement): What is your default partner type? What other qualities interest you?

Chapter 18 (Worlds Colliding): Do you deliberately keep any parts of your life separate from others? Is that healthy for you right now? Why or why not?

Chapter 19 (The Tent Caterpillar): Do you have any "tent caterpillars" eating at you? Is there anyone in your life right now that you need to starve of your emotional energy?

Chapter 20 (My Hero-Worshipping Moth): If you have children, are you doing what you can to help them develop emotionally? How do you help them with their feelings toward their other parent?

Chapter 21 (Hanging Light Fixtures): What new things have you attempted recently? Were you successful? How did it feel to accomplish something?

Chapter 22 (Base Frequency): Can you hear or feel your intuition? What is it saying to you? Do you believe you're on a positive path?

Chapter 23 (The Language of Us): What dictionary do you share with your family and friends? How does that bring you closer?

Chapter 24 (Sorry is an Easy Word to Hate): How do you feel about apologies? Do you say you're sorry too often or not enough?

Chapter 25 (The Ease of Ordinary Things): What do you do well every day? What are your ordinary processes? How are they beautiful?

Chapter 26 (Walls and Bridges): Can you tell when you're putting up walls? How can you put aside fear to build bridges instead?

Chapter 27 (Superfamily): Who is in your superfamily? Why?

Chapter 28 (The Last Jalapeno): Is there anything you do out of kindness that actually delays your emotional growth?

Chapter 29 (Hay Pillows and Splat Corners): Do you believe that the grass is only greener somewhere else? Is it possible to see your current situation differently and create something better?

Chapter 30 (Tubing the Wake): What can you control about your anxieties? How can you keep yourself from feeling overwhelmed? What is your intuition telling you when you feel unsure?

Chapter 31 (The Fly on the Airplane): Is there anything you're avoiding dealing with? Why? How can you benefit from dealing with your issues head-on?

Chapter 32 (The Carousel): Are you afraid of dying? What can you do now to make your life one to be proud of? Why do you think you were put on this Earth at this time in this body?

Chapter 33 (Nine of None): Would you have nine children or none if you had those options? Why?

Chapter 34 (Strings): What strings are on you that you want to be free of? What strings do you put on others? What is the difference between a boundary and a condition?

Chapter 35 (Weed Killer): Do you worry about what other people think? Why? How can you change that thinking?

Chapter 36 (Water Weight): What concerns do you still need to address in your life? What baggage do you need to discard? What's on your bucket list?

Special Thanks

There are so many…

I would like to thank Kristin, my oldest, most talented and beautiful friend, without whom I would not have survived little league, among other things (she makes me say that all the time!). She generously took on the task of managing the editing process for this book and has always helped me in more ways than I ever fully express.

I'm grateful to my siblings and my parents for being supportive of an endeavor as personal as this. I would also like to thank the Bean family for being my family, too.

In addition, I was blessed to have a wonderful focus group that helped me tighten up the message (and the grammar). Joy W., technical editor extraordinaire, Jennifer B., Shannon H., Therese H., Greta K., Lori L., Jennifer L., Carol N., Jill T., Melissa W., Susie W., M.S., and H.C.

For being my guide, for teaching me to trust myself and others, and for believing in me when I couldn't, I owe Zane my undying gratitude.

Finally, I am thankful for the unconditional love and unwavering faith I receive every day from Peter and my children.

References

Andrew Stanton, L. U. (Director). (2003). *Finding Nemo* [Motion Picture].

Goolrick, R. (2009). *A Reliable Wife*. Chapel Hill: Algonquin Books of Chapel Hill.

McMeekin, G. (2000). *The 12 Secrets of Highly Creative Women: A Portable Mentor*. Berkeley: Conari Press.

Pete Docter, D. S. (Director). (2001). *Monsters, Inc.* [Motion Picture].

Townsend, H. C. (1999). *Boundaries in Marriage*. Grand Rapids: Zondervan.

Wise, R. (Director). (1965). *The Sound of Music* [Motion Picture].